This book is dedicated to Caroline, Jodi and Chris.

Together, we journeyed down into the darkness and
uncertainty of the valley of the shadow of death...
then hand-in-hand, we climbed into the brilliant
sunshine to the top of the mountain on the other side.
Our love was, and will always be the rock which
will take us through the rest of the days of our lives.

To all my friends
at Osoyoos United,
I hope you enjoy this.

Best always
Wally

Acknowledgements

To try to put to paper the support my family and I received when things were the bleakest, then to reaching the pinnacle of human emotion and joy, higher itself than Mount Everest, would in itself, be another book.

One does not achieve anything which is fulfilling, by oneself. There are people, events, situations, crises, achievements and dream attainment which all come together to weave a tapestry of emotion and feelings which we know and experience, as life. These moments in time, sometimes minuscule which are gone in a second, or as long as an eternity, affect how we live, hour-by-hour, day-by-day, week-by-week and so on.

Pivotal moments come and are gone in a flash. We must recognize them when they occur. They are often a gift from God. They sometimes manifest themselves innocently, or they can be as a result of a lifetime of planning.

Neither is as important, however, as is *the response.*

That response to each event, is the key to life.

If we shrug them off as being insignificant or having no special meaning when they occur, an emotion, a feeling or an opportunity may be forever lost.

To our relatives and friends in Alberta and British Columbia who arrived in droves during the blistering hot summer of 1994, as I was being decimated by chemotherapy, we thank you. Each visit was another pivotal moment in my healing. For each of you who had a part in this story, thank you - you know who you are.

To the man who was instrumental in saving my life and for my healing, I thank Dr. Jack Chritchley.

I am indebted to the entire medical community in Penticton, especially to all of the wonderful professionals at the Oncology Clinic and lab.

I thank the staff of the Bank Of Montreal where Caroline worked who supported us in so many ways.

Thanks, Dave Bullock, for your support and for believing in me - and allowing me to swim better than you.

And one of my great thrills each Ironman is to stand beside Steve King, the voice of Ironman, on top of that magnificent structure housing the time-clock and finish line. I'm honored to share in announcing Ironman finishers as they cross the line, many who have conquered cancer, heart conditions, other illnesses, diseases and overcome personal tragedies to complete the race.

I thank Graham Fraser the owner of Ironman Canada. Ironman is my metaphor for life. Because of this event which changes lives, there is nothing stopping me from achieving anything I want to. I thank Graham and Kevin MacKinnon, who encouraged me all the way; and for Graham's gracious persmission to use the Ironman Canada logo.

Ironman changed my life dramatically, positively and forever.

To the "army" of Ironman volunteers for helping me get to the finish line when I'd blown out my knee and had to walk the marathon. You are indeed, the heart of this world-class event.

I thank the founding members of the Penticton Writers and Publishers who encouraged me to write this book. Thank you Penny for editing the work and to all the other associate members for your support.

I thank Julie Luoma, Doug Brown and Greg McBryde of lightSPEED Multimedia Inc, for following me around for a year with a video camera prior to Ironman because they believed this was a story that had to be told. They didn't ask for a penny in return. "From Hodgkin's to Ironman" is truly a marvelous piece of work.

Thank you Shelley Daly for the photographs.

To the memory of Ian Mandin who taught me how to "eat the elephant".

To Peter Diggins, my marathon walking partner. A man whom I knew for only six hours, but who helped me change the course of the rest of my life.

To my God, for strength which I felt through every person I knew or met, from those closest to me, to strangers who knew of my struggle and offered me encouragement. The Creator has given me a new lease on life. I'm re-born to inspire others to dream as big as they can be, to strive to achieve their goals, to never give up hope,

...and to never, ever quit!.

FOREWORD

This true story sweeps the reader along a trail of extremes, from a low of severe disability to a triumph of outstanding ability. The book documents the author's physical, psychological, social and financial life as it starts to collapse. This is his world of terror as advanced cancer renders him helpless and dependent. We accompany the author through his struggles against the deep psychological fears that accompany his cancer.

There are messages in this biography for all readers. Fighting cancer is a personal battle and for the patient it is a journey of isolation and loneliness. It is also a journey about determination and the psychological work required to get better. Cancer is destructive and so is the treatment. The treatment is also complex and risky. What happens to survivors? Will a fine precise, infinitely complex instrument like a human being ever be in perfect tune again after colliding with cancer and cancer treatment? There is a story within, that is about community. Who is it that helps mobilize the patient's inner resources to face his illness? How can this disease be managed in a small community? How many professional disciplines need to be coordinated in order for one patient to receive good health care? What has to be in place for the doctor's prescription to become a healing action? Rehabilitation for this victim translated into conquering new fears, and fighting new pains as he challenged the Ironman Canada Triathlon.

This book is a celebration of personal triumphs.

Jack Chritchley,M.D.

IRONMAN CANADA

SWIM COURSE 3.86km (2.4 miles)

MAP SCALE 1 TO 10,000 (metric)
COURSE LENGTH 2.4 miles (3.86 kilometres)

450 METERS

1800 METERS

1612 METERS

LAST HOUSE
AT SAGE MESA

OKANAGAN HIGHWAY NO. 97

KIWANIS
WALKING
PIER

TRANSITION
AREA

S.S. SICAMOUS

OKANAGAN RIVER

LAKESHORE DRIVE

POWER STREET

MARTIN STREET

CITY OF PENTICTON

COMPLIMENTS OF:

STEVEN J. BUZIKIEVICH
PROFESSIONAL LAND SURVEYOR
54 NANAIMO AVE. E.
PENTICTON, B.C.
Phone 492-0559

IRONMAN CANADA BIKE COURSE

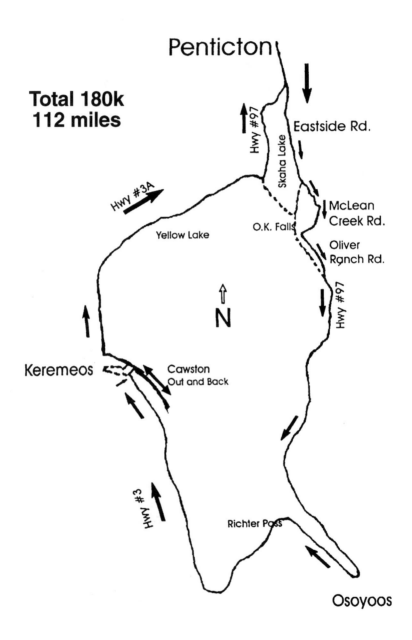

Penticton

Total 180k
112 miles

Hwy #97

Skaha Lake

Eastside Rd.

Hwy #3A

Yellow Lake

O.K. Falls

McLean
Creek Rd.

Oliver
Ranch Rd.

Hwy #97

N

Keremeos

Cawston
Out and Back

Hwy #3

Richter Pass

Osoyoos

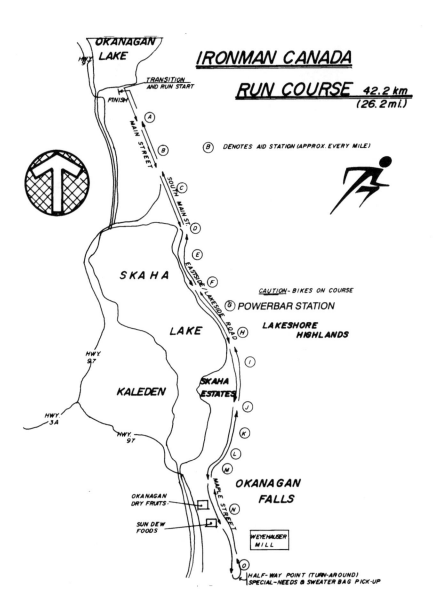

IRONMAN CANADA

RUN COURSE 42.2 km
(26.2 mi.)

OKANAGAN LAKE

TRANSITION AND RUN START

FINISH

MAIN STREET

Ⓐ

Ⓑ Ⓑ DENOTES AID STATION (APPROX. EVERY MILE)

SOUTH MAIN ST.

Ⓒ

Ⓓ

Ⓔ

SKAHA

Ⓕ

EASTSIDE / LAKESIDE ROAD

CAUTION - BIKES ON COURSE

Ⓖ POWERBAR STATION

LAKE

Ⓗ LAKESHORE HIGHLANDS

Ⓘ

HWY 97

KALEDEN

SKAHA ESTATES

Ⓙ

HWY. 3A

HWY. 97

Ⓚ

Ⓛ

Ⓜ

OKANAGAN FALLS

MAPLE STREET

OKANAGAN DRY FRUITS

SUN DEW FOODS

Ⓝ

WEYEHAUSER MILL

Ⓞ HALF-WAY POINT (TURN-AROUND)
SPECIAL-NEEDS & SWEATER BAG PICK-UP

~ 9 ~

Chapter 1

Are you out of your ever lovin' mind?

The question, like a slow-motion, exploding mushroom cloud loomed larger and larger in my head as I lay in bed. Wide awake.

The soft yellow numbers on my bedside digital alarm clock glowed 1:48 a.m.

I could not get it out of my mind. The more I tried to block it out, the more vivid it became. Like a flashing neon light, illuminating, piercing the darkness, the question would not go away.

Do I dare compete in the Ironman Canada Triathlon?

I swung wildly between several emotions; excitement, apprehension, fear, failure, euphoria. I was on the accelerator, then jamming the brakes, lurching forward at break-neck speed, then backward. It would be a long day at work come morning. I took a deep breath, trying to fill every sac in my lungs with air, and let out a long, low sigh so I wouldn't wake my wife, Caroline.

Five hours earlier on September 24th, 1995, we'd been sitting at our kitchen table, firing questions at Dave Bullock, an Ironman Canada Race Society Director. I'd invited him to our house to answer questions about this ultimate triathlon challenge.

The Ironman Canada Triathlon is an extremely popular world-wide event which draws more than 1,700 triathletes from 40 countries to Penticton, British Columbia each August. The race consists of a 2.4 mile swim, followed by a

112 mile bike ride and concludes with a 26.2 mile marathon run.

To earn a finisher's medal, a triathlete must complete the race in under 17 hours.

It is not a typical Sunday stroll in the park carrying a picnic basket filled with fried chicken and cold beer.

Caroline and I had asked many questions of Dave, himself, a two-time Ironman finisher.

I described my own fitness level over the past 25 years to give him an indication as to whether or not he thought I should attempt such a gruelling event.

I had weight-trained, cycled and played hockey on a regular, seasonal basis.

I told him how excited I was, while at the same time expressing my doubts and anxiety about leaving too little time to train for Ironman the following August, only eleven months away.

Dave told us most first-time triathletes at the Ironman distance spent at least two years preparing for the race.

However, in his English accent he told me just before he left, "I believe you can do it, mate." He finished his coffee and we said goodbye. I was even more excited than I had been before we sat down.

But at bedtime, in the darkness, nagging doubts began to surface. Another crucial question, much larger than the others, loomed ominous, with overtones of uncertainty.

Does the fact I nearly died of cancer a year-and-a-half earlier factor into my being able to finish the race?

I was haunted by the thought as I tried to find the sleep which was so elusive.

In February of 1994, I was diagnosed with advanced Hodgkin's disease, a lymphatic cancer, by Dr. Jack Chritchley, one of the most respected cancer specialists in the province. I considered myself fortunate to have been in the right place, at the right time when diagnosed with cancer.

After a lengthy four week battery of exhaustive tests and procedures, he'd carefully staged the degree of Hodgkin's at

3-B, just shy of the final, critical Stage 4. In his examination room, he took me aside after the poking, prodding and blood-work. In his low-keyed, compassionate, caring tone, he told me I was dying of cancer.

But in the same breath, he brightened up, smiled and said, " I want to make you well, so you can work hard and pay lots of taxes."

I knew I could trust this man with my life.

I endured an eight month sentence of harsh, aggressive, body-altering chemotherapy.

Aggressive means you lose your hair, throw up a lot, and get chubby because of the steroids.

I survived, thanks to my faith, family and friends - and a very special oncologist who knew his medicine very, very well.

A few after-effects of the chemotherapy still remained. I only had a partial sense of feeling in my fingers and toes because of the drugs. My tolerance to cold weather was great-ly reduced due to the damage to nerve endings in my digits.

I was thankful we didn't live on the prairies anymore. The icy, winter blasts would have made it impossible and dan-gerous for me to be outside, for even short periods of time. Southern British Columbia is far more forgiving with it's mild winters.

Unable to sleep, my mind took me back to August 26th, 1994 when I was in my sixth month of chemotherapy. I was totally bald, having lost all my hair after the second treat-ment. My muscles had weakened terribly, atrophied from the inability to exercise. My heels, hips, knees and shoulders were inflamed and very sore, because of the chemicals surg-ing through my veins and arteries as they battled the cancer cells.

I could no longer walk normally. I ambled unsteadily on wobbly knees, awkwardly, slowly from side to side, like an old man without a cane.

I was forced to rest every few minutes; my breath came in short, quick, sometimes painful bursts. The X-rays had discovered two large, tennis ball-sized tumors in my chest, one behind each lung. They made breathing difficult. The summer heat, in the high 90's Fahrenheit (high 30 Celsius range), was stifling.

Another side effect caused my belly to bloat from the Prednisone. The steroid was to help maintain my weight and what little strength I had. On my bald head, I wore a battered straw hat. I dressed to the wrists, ankles and neck in the midsummer heat. I'd been ordered by Dr. Chritchley to stay out of the sun, a typical protocol for patients undergoing chemotherapy.

In the Okanagan, staying out of the blazing sun is like being asked to stay out of the cold in Alaska in January.

On that hot, August Ironman afternoon, Caroline, some friends and I were leaning on a temporary fence erected along the street just south of the transition area. It was the point of return after each leg of the event, and the finish line. The triathlon headquarters was a beehive of activity. Thousands of spectators on the grass, sidewalks and portable bleachers cheered for the triathletes.

It was 1 p.m., and some of the professionals were already returning from the bike portion of the race having finished the swim some five hours earlier.

Every muscle in my body ached to be out there. I wanted to feel the wind in my sweat-drenched hair again. Tears welled up in my eyes and the entire scene before me began to swirl in a multitude of colors, out of focus.

I saw myself pulling strongly through the water, pushing hard on each pedal stroke and running until my lungs collapsed, breaking the tape at the finish line.

I turned to Caroline with tears trickling down my cheeks and in a hoarse voice, choked with quivering emotion, said, "I'm going to do this someday."

As I lay in bed, I revisited that moment, forever etched in my mind.

I didn't realize at the time, how watching the 1994 Ironman would be *the* pivotal event which would change the course of the rest of my life.

I looked at the clock again. Two-eleven a.m. I took another deep, long breath, "I hope my sales manager doesn't ask me any hard questions at work," I muttered aloud as I valiantly tried to get to sleep.

Next day I struggled through the morning in a thick fog, trying to clear the cobwebs with as much strong coffee as my stomach could tolerate.

I was feeling quite a bit better by lunchtime and was standing at my desk when I decided to call Dr. Chritchley for his input into my Ironman decision. We had become close because of our love of physical fitness.

I punched the phone number for the cancer clinic and asked for him. In a short time he answered and we exchanged greetings. I hummed and hawed a bit before I finally blurted out, "Jack, do you think I'm crazy to consider training for Ironman?"

Dead silence.

"Hello?" I asked into the receiver.

"I'm here, Wally," he replied.

"What....ah, what do you think?" I again asked a little slower.

"Whheeeeeeewwwww...,." he uttered in a slow, low whistle. I imagined the wheels in his mind turning, trying to find the right words to say.

"You know you're putting me on the spot, don't you?" he asked in his typical, soft-spoken manner. "I really don't know what to say. I know you'd been in very good shape most of your life...." his voice trailed off. Then in a somber tone, he said, "Remember, you *were dying* when I first saw you".

I felt the blood drain from my face as the memories flooded back. My legs buckled under me and I collapsed into my chair. Neither of us spoke for what seemed like an hour.

Suddenly he coughed, startling me. I almost dropped the phone.

"But hey...you beat cancer, didn't you!" he quickly said, his voice suddenly filled with spirit. "Sure...yeah...why not go for it?"

He laughed and I realized I hadn't been breathing for a while. I moved the phone away from my lips and two lungs full of air exploded from my mouth.

I asked him what the next step would be.

"I'll arrange for the pulmonary function study stress test."

"Huh?"

"Oh, it's nothing more than a procedure which will determine if there is any damage to your heart and lungs from the chemotherapy." I asked him about the stress test.

"I'm going to hook several electrodes to your chest and ask you to run until you feel like throwing up." I could imagine the twinkle in his eye, as he told me this bit of news.

"Just think," he added, "you'll be throwing up for a good reason, instead of the chemotherapy."

I laughed long and hard. He gave me a time and date for the test and said goodbye. When I hung up the phone I said, "Guess I'd better find my sneakers and a plastic bucket."

Chapter 2

It felt very strange walking into the hospital. Although it was a positive visit, I was very conscious of the tightness at the back of my throat. The same tightness I'd felt each time I arrived for another chemotherapy treatment the year before. The relationship of hospital and cancer was deeply entrenched in my subconscious. I often swallowed to try to release the tension of knowing I would soon feel like vomiting shortly after the chemicals were released into my veins.

It was September 30th, a week after Caroline and I had met with Dave Bullock. In that seven day time frame, I had spent every waking minute deliberating the decision I'd made. Often I'd find myself daydreaming at my sales desk at the radio station. Meetings with clients and prospects were a blur. I was running, cycling and swimming in my mind.

The excitement ebbed and flowed, back and forth; apprehension, doubt and uncertainty would rise like a tsunami. Euphoria would follow, at the thought of what I was about to embark on.

A few years earlier I would have never dreamed of participating in the Ironman Canada Triathlon.

But then I never thought I'd ever have to face cancer either. I thought back to the previous year when I watched the triathletes during the race. *Those people are in very good shape*, I scolded myself. *What on earth makes you think you can do this?* I though again of the cancer journey and my family. I knew why I would have to do it.

Dressed in my sweatshirt and pants, I entered the east door of the Penticton Regional Hospital at eight o'clock that morning. The hallway to the Pulmonary Ward was empty. I could hear the echo of my sneakers as I walked down the long corridor.

After I checked in at the registration counter, I was ushered into a small room with an array of electronic equipment in which were panels of flashing, digital numbers.

There were wires everywhere. As my eyes scanned the room, I saw the device which would propel my heart and lungs into the stratosphere. In the far corner stood the treadmill. After the preliminary check-up I would get on it and run till I was spent.

The technician arrived and we introduced ourselves. She invited me to sit on a stretcher next to a large diagnostic monitor with wires dangling from it. She asked me to remove my sweatshirt and T-shirt, then lie down.

With a razor, she deftly shaved several small areas of hair from my chest. In minutes, she'd attached seven, one inch band-aid like circular patches, each with an exposed electrode in the center. She hooked up a wire to each and keyed several commands into a computer. She needed to get a resting pulse rate and asked me to relax for a couple of minutes.

Fat chance. I'm about to get onto a treadmill and run until I puke - and I'm supposed to relax?

Lying there, trying to coax my pounding heart to slow down, I thought of the many tests and procedures I'd been subjected to over the last 18 months before, during and after my chemotherapy. I remembered the anxiety and how difficult it was to stay positive, waiting for each result; especially the post-chemo tests.

Waiting to hear if the cancer was gone.

The needles, chemicals, X-rays, cat-scans, bloodwork, Gallium scans, and finally the verdict.

"Pardon?," I asked.

She was talking to me, gently shaking my shoulder. I'd been day-dreaming. "Please sit up. I have the data I need."

I didn't realize Dr. Chritchley had entered the room. "How are you feeling?" he asked grinning, as he firmly shook my hand. His dark eyes sparkled behind his glasses.

It was great to see him again. He'd been such an inspiration throughout the treatments.

His wry, soft-spoken sense of humor helped me through some rough times. Our first meeting seemed like eons ago.

"Okay," he said, "let's have a look," as he picked up his stethoscope.

He asked the usual questions, took my pulse and blood pressure. "Now, let's see how your ticker made it through the chemo. Come over to the treadmill."

I pulled off my nylon sweatpants. Underneath I wore a pair of jogging shorts.

The wires had been removed from the patches on my chest before I left the stretcher.

After I'd stepped on the machine, Dr. Chritchley attached a different set of wires from another, larger machine. It would monitor my vital signs during my time on the treadmill.

I would run until I was exhausted, or until I was told to stop by Dr. Chritchley. He would closely monitor the readings and if he felt I was in danger, he would stop the test.

Almost gingerly I started to move my legs.

"You'll walk for a couple of minutes and then we'll slowly increase the speed," he said.

Two minutes passed by in a flash. The belt picked up speed and I began to jog.

Over the next few minutes, the belt speed increased in small increments and before long, I was running. I looked at the clock above me; 8:53. I'd been in motion for seven minutes.

"How are you feeling?" Dr. Chritchley asked.

"Fine," I blurted out. My breath was coming in short, quick bursts. Beads of perspiration were forming on my forehead.

Dr. Chritchley and the technician were busy at the monitor punching information into a keyboard. I heard electronic sounds as they watched a series of waves on an oscilloscope. I assumed they represented what was happening to my heart.

I was very conscious of the pulse rate monitor which I could clearly see to my right. It had started at 74 beats per minute and was now at 152. I wasn't sure if it should be that high but I was confident if anything was not going well, Dr. Chritchley would abort the test.

It wouldn't look good on his record to have a patient expire on a treadmill.

I looked down. The belt seemed to be going a hundred miles an hour. My old sneakers flashed back and forth. The skin on my shins glistened from the sweat.

I blew some perspiration from my mustache. My eyes began to sting from the salty drops flowing from my scalp. I wiped them with the towel I had around my neck.

8:56. Ten minutes passed. I felt the belt surge again. More speed. My heart hammered in my chest. My lungs were on fire. Spots formed in front of my eyes. I blinked hard, several times, trying to get rid of them. They were now in orbit around my head, spinning slowly, some brighter than the others.

I'd felt like this before, whenever I'd exerted myself too much.

"You okay?" Dr. Chritchley asked. I lied and held up my right thumb. I couldn't speak anymore. I pushed harder. My body was pleading with me to quit.

NO, I WILL NOT STOP!

The sweat, now running in rivulets down the middle of my chest, began to soak the hair. I picked up the plastic water bottle at the front of the treadmill and with my shaking right hand, squeezed a stream of water into my parched throat and an extra shot into my face. The cool water ran down my cheeks and chin to mix with the sweat on my heaving rib cage.

I looked at the clock. 8:59. Thirteen minutes had elapsed. I was running as hard as I could. My hips, knees, and heels were aching. I was conscious of my rapid, coarse breathing.

Again Dr. Chritchley asked if I wanted to continue. He was watching me closely. I nodded, but I knew I was near the end.

I glanced again to my right, my pulse rate showed 162 beats per minute, as high as it was to get.

Just a couple of minutes more, plleeeaaassse.., I begged my body. With every ounce of strength left in me, I put my head down and forced my legs to move as fast as they could.

Finally, at 9:01, I signalled with my right hand that I could no longer continue.

"Great job," Dr. Chritchley exclaimed enthusiastically as the treadmill belt quickly slowed down. His voice sounded disembodied, as if coming from a large, empty oil drum.

When the belt stopped, I staggered off the machine. The room was reeling and undulating. My rubbery legs buckled under me and Dr. Chritchley caught me. My stomach was churning. I felt like throwing up. My chest was heaving rapidly, in and out, as I tried to suck in huge volumes of air. I felt dizzy and steadied myself against him as he removed the wires.

"Quick, come over here and lay down," the technician ordered. "I have to take your pulse to compare it with your resting rate before you started the run."

I collapsed onto the stretcher. She quickly re-attached the original set of wires to the moisture-soaked patches.

"Hold your breath!" she commanded.

"WHAT?" I blurted out.

I was stunned and my mind screamed. *HOLD MY BREATH! ARE YOU OUT OF YOUR MIND, WOMAN?*

I couldn't believe it! My heart was beating a ga-zillion times a minute and she wanted me to stop breathing?

"You MUST try not to breathe so the machine can get a correct reading of your vital signs," she pleaded. "It can only be done between breaths."

I closed my lips tightly - for two seconds. The blood in my temples pounded against my skull. My bursting lungs exploded through my mouth.

"Please try again" she begged.

Finally after four excruciating attempts, she got the reading she needed.

"Great! You can relax now," she smiled.

"How about if I die," I groaned.

"Lay there for a few minutes while we gather all the data," she said.

Slowly, my breathing and heart rate returned to normal as I lay there, soaked in sweat. My hair was glued to my forehead.

I felt a hand on my shoulder and through a fog, I heard Dr. Chritchley's voice tell me what I wanted to hear.

"According to these results, your heart and lungs are in very good shape. There's no evidence of any damage because of the chemotherapy. You can start your Ironman training."

With that he shook my hand vigorously and wished me well. I meekly thanked him, gingerly got up and carefully put my aching legs and feet on the floor. I put on my T-shirt and sweatshirt. They instantly clung to my skin, absorbing the sweat like a sponge.

Slowly I walked out of the room after thanking the technician and made my way down the hallway to the exit. A couple of times I steadied myself on the wall to my right as I staggered down the corridor which gently swayed like the bow of a ship under my feet. The exit seemed a mile away.

Even though Indian summer had settled into the Okanagan, a sudden chill ran up my spine as I left the hospital. I shivered, and quickened my pace as best as I could to my car. I looked at my watch. 9:30. I'd been in there an hour and a half. Unlocking the door, I eased myself into the driver's seat. My joints creaked. I was utterly exhausted. I closed my eyes and thought about my decision - again.

How many hundreds of hours of training would it take? How many thousands of miles of swimming, biking and running lay ahead of me? What about injury? What about the toll it would take on the relationship with my family? How about my job - would it suffer as well?

A barrage of questions blasted me squarely in the face. I wondered if Sir Edmund Hillary thought about these things as he stood looking up at Mt. Everest. I contemplated if Neil Armstrong dwelled on this kind of negative thinking as he stepped from the lunar module.

I shook my head and snapped back to reality.

I wondered if I was wondering too much.

I started the car and put it in gear. Still fending off questions, I decided one of the first things I better do was learn to swim.

Chapter 3

I drove to my sales job each weekday from Penticton to Kelowna, 40 miles north along Highway 97.

The morning sky was usually clear with only a few clouds to the east. Okanagan Lake shimmered in the autumn sunlight to my right as I drove through Summerland, several hundred feet above the sparkling blue water.

The drive allowed me to collect my thoughts for the day, filled with visions of Ironman training. I thought of how the work of Canadian Cancer Society volunteers and research by cancer specialists was paying enormous dividends. I decided I would encourage others by my example of hope and perseverance and that a diagnosis of cancer need not be a death-sentence.

And there always had to be hope.

I remembered staying at the Cancer Lodge in Vancouver in late 1994 for a series of post-chemo check-ups. The Lodge is a facility for patients who are being treated or examined at Vancouver General. I was heartened by the attitude of some, dismayed by others who seemed resigned to a fatalistic outlook on their disease.

The patients with the positive outlooks were cheery, almost radiant, in spite of the obvious side effects of their chemotherapy or radiation treatments. In conversation, they'd spoken in the future tense. Others, shuffled about, head down, walking slowly, as if to their graves. I was determined to never give up, and with my survival, motivate others.

That motivation would start with the Ironman.

At 12:30 pm, during my lunch hour on October 5th, 1995, I took off my shirt, tie and slacks in the men's locker room at the radio station.   I put on an old pair of jogging shorts, T-shirt and sweatshirt. I laced up my old Addidas. Then I reached for my favorite ball cap given to me by friends in Culver City, California several years earlier.

CKOV Radio is located in the south-east edge of Kelowna on Lakeshore Drive in an area known as Mission. It was a mild 60 degree Fahrenheit (16 degree Celsius), sun-filled afternoon as I took my first steps out of the sliding back doors of the lunch room. I walked briskly over the well-manicured lawn, across the paved parking lot and east onto Cooke Street. Around me the low mountains of the beautiful Okanagan valley rose to meet the handful of puffy white clouds in the brilliant blue sky.

Jogging, I picked up the pace and soon came to Gordon Drive, leaving the city behind. North along Gordon, the contrast was striking. To the left, the city; to the right, horses and cows contently grazed in lush green pastures. Bulrushes swayed gently in the deep ditch on my right. Finches dove and rose erratically from unseen nests.

I started a slow run when I felt thoroughly warmed up. A quarter mile north, I turned east on Casorso Street with acreages and hobby farms on both sides of the paved road. The asphalt was the only clue that I wasn't in the middle of a rural community. I picked up my running.

Running is stretching the truth. It was more like a cross between a lope and a jog which I did on purpose. I wanted to start my training slowly and deliberately. I planned on running a couple of miles each time for the first few days, then lengthen the distances.

A pair of cows to my left, near the barbed wire fence, looked absently at me, chewing contentedly on their cud as I ran by, only twenty feet away.

"This is great!" I exclaimed outloud. "Green grass, ditches, farms, birds chirping, fresh air..." I paused and sucked in a large amount of a familiar, pungent odor into my nose..."and I'm jogging in cattle country."

The undeniable odor of cow dung permeated the air. I'd forgotten how difficult it is to run while holding one's breath.

By the time I'd reached the Tee-to-Green golf course, halfway through my run , I was sweating. I'd measured out my jogging route in my car earlier in the week. The golf course was the turn-around. I checked my watch. I'd been jogging for 17 minutes and had covered 1.3 miles.

I was feeling pretty good as I headed back, but noticed my nose was running, my breath, labored and my right ankle was starting to throb. Fifteen years earlier, I'd broken it playing hockey and whenever there was a change in barometric pressure, my foot hurt. I could forecast a change in weather 48 hours ahead of it's arrival.

I'd often limp for a few days until the barometer stabilized.

Just over a half-hour later, I arrived back at the radio station. My hair, T-shirt and shorts were soaked. What had started as an easy two-and-a-half mile run turned into a sweaty 33 minute trial.

I struggled to peel off my soaked clothes. My T-shirt felt like it was glued to my back. I could barely pull it over my head. I stepped into the shower and turned on the hot water. It stung my shoulders but felt so good.

I could not believe I was so badly out of shape. I closed my eyes as the steam swirled around me. In the distance, eleven months away, I saw the image of the Ironman triathlon, I could barely make it out. But I knew as I got closer to the race, it would loom larger, and more ominous.

Again I questioned my decision to do the race.

I sat down in the shower stall because my legs were suddenly weak. A shiver recoiled through my torso, from the base of my neck to the lower back in spite of the hot, stinging water spraying onto my head.

I'd experienced the same sensation in the past, when I felt I may have bitten off more than I could chew. Then I remembered what a close friend, Ian Mandin, once told me when we'd talked about challenges we'd each faced at different times in our lives.

He grinned and told me, "A challenge in life is like eating an elephant. Do you know how to eat an elephant?" he asked. I shook my head in ignorance.

He answered, "One bite at a time."

I'd never forgotten what he told me, and it was often a comfort when I'd faced a difficult time in my life, or if I questioned my ability to complete a task.

The same doubts again crept into my mind; the ones from that fateful meeting at our kitchen table a couple of weeks earlier.

Will I be able to do this with only eleven months of training? What about injury?

CAN I DO IT?

I knew my mental preparation was equally as important as my physical training. My body would be challenged like never before. My mind also had to fortify itself to prevent the negative thoughts from cracking my armor of confidence.

I had roughly 330 days to get ready. As I dried off and got dressed, I could feel the stiffness begin to get in my legs. I knew I'd feel the consequences of my initial first day of training the next morning. A smile, however, formed at the corners of my mouth.

I had taken the first very small bite of my monstrous elephant.

Chapter 4

My legs felt like two concrete pillars when I woke up the next morning. I couldn't remember the last time I experienced that kind of soreness. I groaned as I slowly, stiffly, and with considerable difficulty, swung my legs over the side of our waterbed.

I planted my feet 36 inches apart and gently stood up. For a moment I stood there, *Okay, let's see what I feel like.* I took a step.

I sucked in my breath as a blinding flash of pain shot up my legs. *That hurts,* my mind screamed. My calves, hamstrings and lower back signalled I'd over-done my first run. I hobbled slowly to the shower and with my hands, lifted each leg into the tub until I stood under the showerhead and turned on the water. I tried to massage my thighs and calves under the stream of hot water.

With difficulty, I towelled off and penguin-walked slowly back to the closet. I picked out a pair of slacks and a shirt and started to dress. After I'd buttoned up the shirt, I tried to put on my pants. I couldn't lift my feet. I called Caroline to help me get dressed.

I leaned forward, my arms outstretched and placed my hands on my dresser. Caroline squeezed in between, holding my open pants in front of me. Gingerly, I placed each leg into them. She couldn't stop giggling. The humor was lost on me at that moment. .

The next day the soreness was worse. I gritted my teeth every time I got in and out of my car. I wished for an office job. On the third day, I knew I had to get back into my runners. I left the station again, goose-stepping for the first 15 minutes until my legs responded and I could run normally. I'd trained enough over the previous two decades to know the first three weeks of getting back into shape are the most difficult. As I had in the past, I'd sworn to never let myself get out of shape again.

I found I was swearing at myself frequently.

Two weeks later at the end of October, I felt much better and the weather also, was absolutely gorgeous. The Okanagan valley was a blaze of colors, from dark greens to vivid shades of orange and yellow as the leaf-bearing trees began their annual shut-down of chlorophyll production.

I slowly stretched out my running distances. I did a minimum of three miles a day during my lunch hour, Monday through Friday.

I got back on blades again every weekend with my hockey buddies. We played every Friday night in Penticton from 10 to 11:30. I was told hockey was excellent cross-training for the triathlon.

It was time to get into the pool because learning to swim was my first priority. Not only had I never learned to swim, I had not been in water over my head. Ever. During the Ironman swim, at it's furthest point from the beach, the lake is 80 feet deep one mile from shore.

Does wonders for my confidence.

If I couldn't get through 2.4 miles of Okanagan Lake in less than 2 hours, 20 minutes at the end of August, it would be a very short Ironman day.

I enrolled in a beginner's adult swim at the Parkinson Recreation Center in Kelowna at the end of October. I was one of ten students, the only male.

The instructor's name was Marilyn, a pleasant woman in her late 40's, who swam like a fish. She worked with me extensively during the sessions, realizing I was a special case.

I couldn't do simple things like put my face under water and blow bubbles.

What's that Marilyn...tread water?...are you kidding?

Expecting me to breathe and swim at the same time would be a miracle. I sputtered and coughed a lot, and always seemed more under the water than on it.

I was told a couple of very disturbing facts from her which made me even more unsure of my ability to learn to swim.

All things being equal, men have denser bone mass than women, and women have more natural body fat. As a result, women can float better than men. I was convinced I didn't have bone marrow. Instead, mercury coursed through my legs and arms. I floated like a brick.

Little wonder I was exhausted when I occasionally managed to splash my way to the far end of the pool. Standing in four feet of water, I looked forlornly at the deep end, 25 meters from me. It seemed much farther away, as far away as Japan is from Vancouver, or Los Angeles from New York.

I ingested enough chlorinated water to never require a dental visit for the rest of my life. Three weeks and ten classes later, I was no further ahead in my quest to stay on top of the water. I put 'learning to swim' on the back burner and concentrated on my running.

On November 2nd, after a five minute stretch of my calf and thigh muscles, I did a 4.5 mile run. In brilliant sunshine, I worked up a dripping sweat. Most of the soreness was no longer evident in my legs and I usually felt only a twinge of discomfort the following day. In the shower, I did my post-run stretch which felt wonderful. With the steam surrounding me, I worked out the kinks.

It was when I was alone in the shower, that disturbing and negative thoughts occasionally crashed into my mind. I'd feel a sudden stab of panic and a voice in my head screamed out - again, *You can't do this. What makes you think you can possibly finish the race?*

The 'black thoughts' of my life and death struggle still lingered deep in the recesses of my memory. I wasn't sure if they'd ever go away.

But as these dark images invaded my mind, I violently shook my head and shouted out loud, "NO! I will not give in. I will not quit! I've come back from the ultimate battle of life versus death. I CAN DO THIS! <u>I WILL DO THIS!</u>"

Each day, I vowed to run just a little harder, a little farther. Even when my lungs were ready to burst and I felt I couldn't take another step, I would bear down and force my legs to go another hundred yards.

In the middle of November I was told about a Tuesday and Thursday noon-time mens' recreational drop-in hockey hour at the Rutland Arena in north-west Kelowna. Since I had several clients and prospects in that area, I decided to make this part of my training schedule.

My station wagon began to smell like a hockey dressing room.

Caroline bought me a car freshener. It didn't help.

My car stunk like sweaty pine trees.

Chapter 5

On Wednesday morning, November 8th, I arrived at the office of Dr. Jeff Harries, our family physician to get a flu shot. We joked about my Ironman training.

It was Jeff who had requested the blood and urine samples two years earlier which led to my diagnosis of Hodgkin's disease. He'd become a friend and a positive influence.

"You're really serious, aren't you?" he asked.

"You bet!" I exclaimed. I rolled down my sleeve after the shot, put on my sports jacket and said goodbye. The force of my retort surprised me. I thought about it as I got into my car and drove to work. I knew a big part of my preparation was to maintain a positive attitude.

More important than my physical condition, would be my mental capacity to get through the training. It would have to be the same attitude which helped me beat cancer.

Some people openly questioned whether I was serious when they learned I was training for the triathlon. I resigned myself there would be doubters who didn't think it was possible for me to finish. I vowed each one of these 'doubting Thomases' would be another reason for me to complete the race.

The weather was grey, cloudy and cool near the first weekend of November with overnight lows dipping to a few degrees below freezing. Typically the Okanagan winters are dreary, but temperatures are not as cold as on the prairies, or the north-central part of the continent.

I got a membership at Gold's Gym and did my orientation of the equipment. I'd weight-training for 20 years and the experience of a gym was not new to me. I was shown how to use the machines and finished my first session on a treadmill. I ran slowly for five minutes, then incrementally upped the speed of the belt which rolled below my feet. Red flashing numbers indicated the speed and distance on a digital board on the front of the machine It was very clinical running. There were no curbs, uneven ground, gopher holes, gravel, wires or any other natural or man-made hazard to contend with when running outdoors.

I missed the cooling wind to confront me, or push me from behind. As a result, I sweated profusely. The signs on the wall in front of us spelled out, 'please bring towels when using machines.'

The row of nine treadmills faced a large bank of ceiling-to-floor glass through which I saw people playing tennis in a large, warehouse-sized facility with four courts. It was difficult to run and watch tennis at the same time, especially if a game was exciting.

The belt under my runners was only two feet wide on a metal base. More than once I felt the outside of my runners come down on the stationary part of the platform causing me to stumble as I strayed from the center of the belt. It was a lesson in concentration.

On Thursday November 7th, the first big blizzard of the winter hit the valley. Because we weren't supposed to get 'real' winter in the Okanagan, very few motorists were prepared for the icy blast. Traffic snarled to a sliding, fender crunching stop in the middle of the near white-out conditions. Six lanes of vehicles jammed Harvey Avenue from Highway 33 to the floating bridge. Snowploughs and sanding trucks were unable to move. The wail of sirens were almost drowned out by the howling wind.

I knew I could not make it home that night.

Because I kept a wardrobe of suit jackets, slacks and clean shirts at the radio station, I was able to spend the night at the home of Paul and Barb Willis in Rutland. They'd been friends for 25 years. I phoned Caroline and told her I was snowed in.

"Great, isn't it," she said. "We spent our lives on the prairies and you were always able to make it home in the winter if you were out of town. Here we are in Lotusland, and you can't make the thirty mile drive home." We chuckled at the irony.

I continued my daily running sessions at Gold's and decided against working out with the weights. I'd suffered separations on both shoulders in the past 20 years playing hockey. With my three-times-a-week ice times, they were painful, especially the right shoulder.

I constantly found myself sore. My calves, heels, Achilles tendons, thighs, hamstring, groin, elbows and neck - not to mention the shooting pain in my shoulders after hockey, made me walk like I was disjointed.

I'd met with Dr. Chritchley again to let him know how the training was going and he cautioned me of the enormous strain I was placing on my immune system. The very system, which only 20 months earlier, had been annihilated because of the chemotherapy.

I was frequently blowing my nose and I knew I was taxing my immune system to the limit.

Runny noses and playing hockey are not a good match. On the ice, I used the 'farmer's blow' to clean out the nasal passages. One takes a finger, holds it against a nostril and blows forcefully out of the other, then the process is reversed. Because I wear a shield on my helmet, this became a quick precise maneuver to lift the plastic up just enough to clear the stream of mucus. The odd time however, I blew just before I lifted. The resulting mess on the inside of the plastic necessitated a trip to the dressing room for clean-up purposes.

Caroline often told me how disgusting the process was.

"Can't you keep Kleenex's at the bench or dressing room?" she once asked.

I tried to imagine what the other guys would say if I brought a box of tissues to the bench. My masculinity would have certainly been questioned. She dropped the issue and I increased my daily intake of vitamin C.

As I was driving to the rink one morning, I was suddenly struck by something of profound significance.

I was paralleling my chemotherapy journey.

My present trek would take about the same amount of time, but would have a dramatically different ending. Where life itself was uncertain before, this journey would end in a celebration of immense joy when I completed the Ironman.

It would be the fitting, final chapter.

Where I was once terribly weakened, sadly out of shape and flabby because of the steroids, my lungs, heart, legs and upper body were strong and well, and I would be in the best physical shape of my life.

Three days later on Friday, November 10, another blizzard hit with the same savage fury as the one on the previous Tuesday. Because it was the weekend, I took my chances and drove back to Penticton. In my 34 years of driving, I had never seen such a vehicular mess. It took an hour-and-a-half just to get to the bridge from downtown Kelowna, a distance of one mile. The heavy, wet snow melted and turned into a thick, slushy quagmire.

I inched my coupe toward the bridge in the middle lane on Harvey Avenue. The inside of the car was toasty warm, the heater at full blast and I was unusually calm and patient. The daily 100 mile drive had done wonders for my lack of patience in traffic. The radio gave the traffic reports, recommending I stay off the roads.

Great advice - just what I want to hear in the middle of six lanes of traffic in the middle of thousands of cars in a blizzard.

My left ear had been plugged much of the afternoon after my swim and I tilted my head to the left and gave my ear a thump with the palm of my hand. Several more times, I tried to get the ear to pop. A buzz in the canal was annoying and my equilibrium was off.

It seemed to take forever but traffic finally crawled over the bridge and as we slowly turtled to the right up a long, steep hill on Highway 97, I came upon an awesome sight.

Like a giant would throw a handful of dinky-toys on the ground, cars, trucks and semi-trailers were strewn and jack-knifed up the slippery slope. My calmness instantly left me, replaced by a sudden chilling need to be very awake and aware.

One lonely RCMP cruiser and a single tow truck sat helplessly in the middle of the chaos, with red, blue and amber flashing lights, illuminating the snow-lit blackness like a laser light show at a rock concert. The howling wind, blowing snow and swirling exhausts created a surreal, nightmarish scene.

Three hours later, exhausted but thankful for minor miracles, I arrived home. The discomfort in my ear had become a pounding sensation. The ear was totally plugged. I didn't want to take a chance on infection, so after I got home and assured Caroline I was okay, I drove to emergency at Penticton Regional Hospital and had the attending physician look at the ear. He noted some redness, said it wasn't infected and gave me some anti-bacterial ear drops.

It was ten o'clock by the time I got back home. I knew I couldn't play hockey that night. Besides, my fingers still felt like they had a death-grip on the steering wheel, and they probably wouldn't fit into my gloves.

I felt much better the next morning and Caroline and I headed for Spokane, Washington on a weekend trip we'd been planning for a couple of months.

Arriving back home on the Remembrance Day Monday and after unpacking, I did my longest run to date.

It was a cold, blustery day. The wind from the south blasted me full in the face.

Whitecaps formed on foot-and-a-half waves which pounded into the sand as I ran west on the road parallel to Skaha Beach.

I had begun to experience 'runner's high', about 40 minutes into my runs. The phenomenon makes you feel like you can run forever. Breathing slows and running becomes rhythmical and you become oblivious to the surroundings.

But it didn't last forever.

Back home, reality hit like a ton of bricks.

My calves ached and my lungs were sore after sucking in the cold air. I was pleased, however because I'd covered 6 miles in an hour and ten minutes. A month into my training and I'd done a quarter marathon.

By the middle of November, the weather had dramatically taken a turn for the better. The snow had disappeared and by the 18th, the daytime temperatures were in the 50 Fahrenheit (10 degrees Celcius) range.

I picked up a road bike from Chris Prowse at the Bike Barn in Penticton. It was his contribution for my Ironman effort. On my tri-bike, I took its maiden voyage from my house to Okanagan Falls and back, some 20 miles. It was 4:30 p.m. when I left. The sun slowly sank behind the mountains to the west. I was wearing my nylon sweat pants, a sweatshirt and no gloves. As I cycled south on East Side Road along the shore of Skaha Lake it was warm, the temperature about 52 Fahrenheit (12 degrees Celcius).

On the way back, the sun had disappeared and the light breeze from the lake suddenly turned cold and hit me full-force in the face. It would be a struggle to get back home. I wished I'd thought ahead enough to have taken a jacket and gloves with me. The chill permeated my fingers, nose and ears, and when the sun goes went down in the mountains, darkness falls in a hurry. I could see the streetlights of the south end of the city, a half-dozen miles ahead of me.

My hands were like blocks of ice; tears from the cold, rolled down my cheeks. My vision was blurred. A compounding factor manifested itself again that afternoon as my intolerance to cold became a painful reality.

Darkness had set in when I arrived home an hour later and admonished myself because it's not safe to be cycling at night without lights. When I got inside, my nose and eyes were dripping and running, the feeling totally gone in my finger-tips and toes, and my ears were the color of ripe tomatoes.

I stripped off my sweats with enormous difficulty because my fingers were so numb. I ran a hot bath as I fumbled to remove my sweatshirt. Gingerly, I stepped into the steamy mist circling around me. The hot water on my icy toes and fingers made me cry out in pain. I gritted my teeth and sat down. I was surprised at how cold my butt was. It burned as I reached the bottom of the tub. Inch-by-inch, I submerged my body till I was in water up to my chin.

As I lay in the delicious heat of the water, I made a mental note of two things I must do in the future when biking in cool weather.

I would not go out without gloves, ear protectors and a jacket until the following spring and I would make sure to ride only in the daylight.

It's not cool to have lights on a triathlon bike.

Chapter 6

Sunday November 19th, dawned sunny with a forecast high of 54 degrees Fahrenheit (12 degrees Celsius). I had planned a seven mile run. I didn't know it at the time, but that event would prove the critical importance of eating enough food two hours before a lengthy or strenuous work-out.

In the mid 1980's , I had been diagnosed as being hypo-glycemic, a condition of low blood sugar, with symptoms similar to a diabetic reaction.

If I didn't eat frequently enough, especially when training, I would get the shakes, feel drained, panicky, disoriented and ill. I was well aware of my condition before I took off for my run at 2:45 p.m., almost four hours since brunch at 11 that morning. Caroline dropped me off near Okanagan Falls, seven miles from our house, and I'd planned to run back home.

Fifty minutes into the run, at the six mile mark, I began to feel squeamish. I fought off waves of panic and illness. I tried to remain focused, to ignore the sick feeling which ebbed and flowed and I forced my shaky legs to keep moving. I strug-gled through the ugly sensation enveloping me, as the blood sugar level plummeted.

Shaking and sweating profusely, I arrived at our front door an hour and eight minutes after starting the run. Caroline was putting the finishing touches on a roast beef dinner. She took one look at me and knew I was in trouble, and quickly ushered me to the table. She'd seen me 'hit the wall' before and knew exactly what I needed. I inhaled a plate of mashed potatoes, gravy, meat and vegetables. Ten minutes later, I began to feel better.

Back in the steam of another hot bath, I admonished myself again, and made a mental note to keep strict track of when I ate, and to back-time my eating whenever I would do a lengthy training session.

A few days later on a Friday morning, I reached down to turn on the shower, and suddenly got dizzy. I felt like I was getting the flu. I ached all over and my stomach felt tight.

I knew, however, it was more than the illness; there was another reason why I was not feeling well.

I was not resting enough between training sessions.

I'd felt drained and fatigued for several weeks, and was warned by my triathlon friends about the importance of accepting days off as a vital, integral part of my training. I'd ignored their advice - till that day.

Reluctantly, I took a week off training.

The following seven days proved to be one of the most difficult times since I began running in October. I fought back the intense desire to get into my running gear and head out on the road. Whenever I saw someone running or cycling, I swallowed hard and looked away. An enormous sense of guilt overtook me. I knew however, the period of self-imposed rest was necessary if I was to achieve my goal.

I was feeling much better on the 27th and got back into my sweats and runners and did a short four mile run. I clipped my portable cassette player to the belt of my bottleholder and inserted a tape of my favorite rock classics and headed backwards through time. Running allowed me to clear my head, to put things in perspective. I ran in a methodical, mechanical motion, deeply immersed in my thoughts. I didn't think about style or breathing properly.

I had many hours to fill during the long runs, and I often thought about 'what ifs'. I reflected on how my life had unfolded over the past half-century. I'd applied to enter the Faculty of Education at the University of Calgary in late 1968, desiring to be a Physed Teacher. I'll never know why I didn't follow through. Perhaps it was because jobs were plentiful in the late 60's and I didn't like the idea of four more years of school, so I went to work instead.

Two years of working in a warehouse changed my tune.

In 1970, I was accepted into the Television, Stage and Radio Arts Program at the Southern Alberta Institute of Technology in Calgary. My broadcasting career took me through 24 years in rock'n'roll and country music radio, a battle with cancer and an intimate journey through the valley of the shadow of death.

Reality exploded in front of me as I returned to the present. I knew I must not think about "what if's". I had to live in the present and to let the past remain where it was.

As winter entrenched itself, I took more time to carefully stretch before every run or hockey game. I often iced my right shoulder after each session. A chronic, nagging groin pull necessitated a lengthy stretching of my upper leg muscles.

Temperatures plummeted to well below freezing by December first and I was back on the treadmill in the gym.

In the three weeks before Christmas, I worked harder and longer during each workout and took every third day off. I booked a half-dozen physiotherapy sessions for my shoulder. The soreness subsided and the nagging muscle and joint injuries felt better after the treatments .

During the Christmas season, we celebrated with family and friends. As I spent time with my wife, daughter and son, I thought back again to what Dave Bullock had told me about the critical importance of having the support of my loved ones.

I could not be selfish. They were equally as important in this daily equation of juggling work, training, and time together. Without their love, support, and encouragement, it would all be futile. I swore never to take them for granted and to think of them each time I began a workout.

My brother Wolf, his wife Corine, son, Ryan and daughter, Heather arrived from Salmon Arm on December 24th. As we shared our gift opening on Christmas morning, I looked around me at the discarded wrapping paper, the gifts scattered under the tree and gave a silent prayer of thanks.

We feasted on the traditional turkey, mashed potatoes and gravy, not to mention the sweet goodies during the Yuletide. I loved it as I was trying to eat at least 4,000 calories a day.

It was an enviable task. *Work as hard as you can, and eat constantly.*

When they left on Boxing Day, we started gearing up for our family vacation to Hawaii. Visions of sand, surf, beaches, deep-tanning oil and pineapples danced in my head. We'd planned this holiday for more than a year. It would be the last we took as a family because our kids were in their late teens and would soon be going their own way.

On December 28th, I did a 'maintenance' run and swim. They were low impact, light workout sessions which kept my muscles limber. I ran on the treadmill at the gym but it was an abysmal, wasteful attempt. I was tired from lack of sleep because of the holidays. In my hurry, I didn't stretch properly and I hurt my right calf muscle. The rest of the workout was no better. When I got to the pool and into my swimsuit, I realized I'd left my ear and nose plugs in the car. With a half-foot of snow on the ground and the temperature at 16 degrees Fahrenheit (minus 10 Celsius), I didn't feel like tip-toeing almost naked to my car to get them. In the pool, I couldn't put my head under water so I did only a dozen lengths using the breast stroke, then hit the showers.

Again, I mentally spanked and berated myself for not being prepared.

I was fortunate the mind police couldn't hear because I'd be in trouble for self-mental abuse.

Chapter 7

On December 31st, I closed out the year with my longest run, eight miles in one hour, twenty minutes. I could've gone another 15 or 20 minutes, but the soreness in my right groin caused me to stop when I did.

I also suffered from 'nipple rash'. This painful condition arose when my perspiration-soaked T-shirt under the sweatshirt or jacket rubbed against my nipples in very cold weather.

I learned quickly from the other triathletes to coat them in Vaseline which prevented the rash.

I'm not sure if this is a gender-specific condition but I certainly wasn't about to ask any female athlete I knew if it was also something she might have experienced.

I also re-discovered a very interesting physiological occurrence affecting the male of the human species. When a man engages in outdoor pursuits in very cold weather, a phenomenon takes place. The genitals, in their desire to escape the frigid, blustery winter wind whistling through the crotch of the jogging pants, try to force their way back up into the warmth of the pelvis, closer to the core of the body heat. I think it has something to do with the survival of the species.

Urinating is next to impossible immediately after a run in sub-zero temperatures.

I stuffed a facecloth down the front of my underpants before putting on my jogging pants when I ran in the cold. It helped a bit. I thought, surely in Canada, someone could invent a battery-powered genital warmer. It could make one rich. I chuckled when I thought of the required testing before it could be CSA approved. And what would the TV commercial look like? What about actors, and the announcer? I giggled all the way home in the cold, thinking of the possibilities.

"...and now for the rugged outdoor man, K-Tel presents..." I burst out laughing.

That night, we celebrated a quiet New Year's Eve with the kids with our traditional year end fondue.

Four days later, after lunch, we piled into our Cavalier Z-24 coupe and headed for Vancouver, 250 miles away.

Through snow, ice and fog, we reached our destination about 6 p.m and checked into our hotel. Next morning, we arrived at the airport at 6:30, yawning because we'd been too excited to sleep. Dreams of playing in the warm Pacific waters just a few hours away kept us from dozing off. Jodi's stomach produced butterflies the size of pigeons so we gave her some medication to calm her nerves. We were ushered into the plane and right on time at 8:30 a.m., the gigantic 757 rumbled down the runway and blasted off for Hawaii.

Six hours later, we arrived in Honolulu. The warm, humid air of this Pacific paradise wafted around us as we stepped from the aircraft. In a whirlwind of typical, tourist activity, we visited the famous sites we'd always seen pictures of, and read about. For two days we saw the island, posed for pictures, and ate pineapples. It was a constant blur of activity, and several times a day we heard from the driver, "get on the bus", "get off the bus".

On our third and final day in Honolulu, we went to Waikiki to spend the day on the beach. As we lay on the sand, surrounded by hundreds of sun-worshipers, a bronzed, blue-eyed hippie throw-back from the 60's strolled past us and asked if anyone wanted to learn to surf. He introduced himself as "Indiana".

My heart leaped into my throat. "Kawabunga!", I said. "Show me the way to your surfboard, man".

Caroline quickly got up on her elbows and gave me a frightened look. Indiana nonchalantly waved his hand at her and assured us, none of his students had drowned and he wasn't about to break that streak. Reluctantly, she agreed.

Like a 16 year old, I jumped to my feet in that hot Hawaiian sand, shook his hand and excitedly said, "let's go!" I followed him with five other neophyte surfers a couple of hundred yards down the beach to a row of surfboards sticking straight up on a rack like missiles about to be launched.

Indiana had left California for the Hawaiian islands in 1972 as a 21 year old looking for work. I quickly did the math - he was 45. He settled at Waikiki, bumming around day-to-day, teaching tourists to surf, at $25 dollars a lesson.

What a life, forty-five going on 18, in the land of perpetual sun, surf and palm trees.

I felt a twinge of envy as I looked into his deeply set blue eyes surrounded by wavy, bleached-blonde locks and a golden-brown tan. My skin screamed out it's delicate, tourist whiteness, next to him.

Again, almost with reverence, I looked at the line-up of surfboards, each about eight feet long. I had yearned to learn to surf since I visited southern California in 1968, after high school graduation.

I imagined grabbing one of Indiana's board's under my arm, tearing down the beach toward the breakers, my hair blowing in the salty air, aiming the tip of the missile into the crashing surf to challenge the twenty to thirty foot swells.

As my heart hammered in wild anticipation, all the Beach Boys surf songs I'd ever hummed while land-lubbering on the prairies whirled through my brain. "Surfin' USA", "California Girls", "Catch a Wave", "Surfin'", and a myriad of others blared into my head.

I thought, *this is great cross-training for Ironman - too bad they don't have a surf portion of the triathlon. It would be a great excuse to come here more often.*

Reality quickly crashed down around me.

For an hour the boards lay flat, dry-docked on the sand, as Indiana carefully instructed the six of us on how to properly get up on a surfboard.

We laid face down on the boards and on his command, grabbed the sides, quickly brought our feet up under our hips. In a fluid-like motion, we pushed straight up with our arms, and in a crouch, spread our feet, shoulder-width apart, one to the tip of the board, the other to the rear.

Simple stuff.

He showed us how to wax the board. I found out why male surfers shaved their chests. The wax was a thick, candle-like substance shaped like a bar of soap which stuck like glue. When I got up practicing my first stance, I left several chest hairs in the sticky goop. It felt like someone had ripped a big bandage from my torso.

Indiana taught us a couple of other basic rules. He showed us how to protect ourselves from injuring our necks if we were thrown off the board and how to dismount the board in the ocean without losing it.

"Ready guys?", Indiana asked suddenly. "It's time to catch a wave."

My eyes glazed over. I was breathing hard. I could feel my heart beating in my temples.

This is it!

The old refrain boomed in my head; *...let's go surfin' now, everybody's learning' how....*

We picked up our boards and followed Indiana to the water. Waikiki Beach unfolded in front of us. Hundreds of swimmers and surfers bobbed in the surf.

Like a string of ducklings following their mother, we lined up behind him, lay on our boards and paddled a couple of hundred yards into the Pacific.

Straddling his surfboard, he barked instructions. "Turn your boards back toward the shore and paddle like hell when I shout". We were surrounded by three foot swells. Suddenly I was thankful they weren't any higher. My nerves were tingling, my throat dry. Six feet below me through the clear water, lay the light brown sandy bottom.

"Go - Go - Go!", Indiana suddenly shouted.

I looked behind me at a small wave forming. Furiously I paddled. The board knifed through the water, the tip rising.

"Get up - Get up!", he screamed.

Smoothly, just as I'd been taught, I lifted my butt and swung my legs up under me. I let go of the sides and stood up, textbook perfect - for two seconds.

On that surf board, it felt like I was standing on a swing in a playground with nothing to hang on to. The board suddenly turned into two thousand pounds of raging bull. It went this way and that; up and down; back and forth, undulating, bucking and twisting.

The last thing I saw before I was unceremoniously flipped backwards into the Pacific, was my board launching itself into the air, just like at mission control in Florida.

My hands touched bottom and I pushed myself to the surface. In the rush of the moment, I sucked in a mouthful of water. The salty taste gagged me. I spat it out and tried to rid my mouth of the bitterness.

I swam back to my board and had difficulty getting back on because of the wave motion. It took a dozen attempts, but I finally caught a nice wave, and...I was surfing!

In a slight crouch, my knees bent, feet parallel to the board, arms out at my sides and my body facing the beach, I was riding the wave.

The exhilaration was unexplainable. I kept the board under control, weaving to the left, then right to maintain my balance as I picked up speed.

LOOK AT ME!, I wanted to scream. *I'M SURFING!*.

The surfboard picked up more speed as the wave grew and started to curl. The euphoria was suddenly shattered as I looked in horror at a young man on a board, oblivious to me, paddling directly into my path, about fifty or sixty yards in front of me.

I panicked. What a way to start a vacation! Impaling some-one on the tip of a surfboard. How would I explain this to the cops? Would the blood attract sharks?

It would be tough on the police trying to explain to my wife and kids, how the great white shark took two hapless surfers to their early demise.

I remembered the emergency dismount that Indiana had taught us. I quickly jumped off the board to my left and grabbed it tightly. Seconds later, the surfer jolted upright when he saw me. We almost touched the tips of our boards as we crossed paths.

My temper flared and I cursed him under my breath. *I could've ridden that wave right to the beach!* I rode several more after that, but none of them compared to the one that got away.

Exhausted, after four hours in the water, I dragged the board back to the stand and thanked Indiana for the experience.

Just before we left the beach for our flight to Maui, I looked back at the ocean, my heart swelling with emotion. I'd taken another bite out of the elephant in my journey to Ironman by attempting and conquering something I'd dreamed of doing since the 1960's.

We flew to Maui in a 737 to explore the island which had been so highly recommended by friends who'd been there before. We picked up our rented car at the airport and drove to our hotel in Lahaina, a town on the west side of the island. We spent the next seven days marvelling at the palm trees and exotic vegetation we'd only seen in the travel brochures. We snorkeled at the Molokini crater, drove the road to Hana and saw the Seven Pools.

Lahaina's easy pace was just what we desired after the busy lifestyle in Honolulu. Caroline and I were surprised at how well the kids co-existed with us in this laid-back atmos-phere. Jodi was 17 and Chris, 19.

I ran six of the ten days we were there, and discovered a very interesting phenomenon. Because of the heat and humidity, I didn't need to warm-up or stretch. I began with a slow jog, and within five or ten minutes I was running at a good, steady pace. I found the warmth absolutely invigorating. Because of my cold intolerance, the climate was perfect for me.

When I did my first run, I spent most of the time marvelling at the surroundings.

The Pacific Ocean sparkled in the sun to my left about a hundred yards away. I could smell the deliciousness of the sea air. A slight breeze in my face parted my hair. In no time I was sweating. The temperature was 88 degrees Fahrenheit (33 degrees Celsius) when I left the motel room about 4 p.m. I ran under palm trees, around and through a variety of tropical plants. The old, narrow sidewalks of Lahaina melted away behind me under my joggers. Passing the north end of the town, I was running easily, effortlessly. I ran northward on the side of the highway facing traffic.

The absence of pain in my knees, hips and heels because of the heat and humidity was starkly evident. I loved it. It was like a new-found elixir. I wanted to ask Caroline if we could move to Maui. Maybe I could convince her to do it for medical purposes. I'm sure I could get our family doctor to prescribe it.

The gorgeous Hawaiian sunset began to manifest itself with a multitude of colors and cloud formations of incredible magnitude in the western skyline. An explosion of oranges and red hues against the darkening late afternoon sky surrounded by pillowy clouds, melted into the vividly striking green grass. Like a gigantic unseen artist at work, the Creator painted a masterpiece of nature in it's majestic, encompassing beauty which unfolded before me as I ran.

I found myself out of breath, not from running but from trying to absorb the dazzling beauty in which I was a participant. I felt I could run forever. I'd consumed two bottles of water, and an hour and seven miles later, I arrived back at the hotel. My hair was soaked; my T-shirt glued by perspiration to my back. The sweat rolled off my eyebrows, nose and chin and splashed to the pavement. I thought how wonderful it would be to qualify for the Ironman Triathlon World Championship in Kona each year in October.

My emotions were bursting. I was running on strong, healthy, tanned legs; never feeling better. Tears filled my eyes, mixing with the sweat on my cheeks as I remembered the chemotherapy. After a cool shower, we ate supper which we barbecued on a grill outside our hotel.

Great holidays always flash by. On the day before we left, we drove back to our favorite beach at Kihei, thirty miles south to spend the late morning and afternoon. The waves were usually six to seven feet high but because of a tropical storm near the islands a few days earlier, some monster waves were created; some as high as 15 feet. In awe, we stood on the beach and watched as the whole ocean seemed to rise up in front of us, then we heard the thunderous crash as each gigantic wave hammered into the ocean floor. It sent boiling foam and churning water five or six feet high onto the shore at our feet.

We'd rented boogie boards and a VHS camera. Boogie boards are made of styrofoam, about four feet long and approximately the width of a surfboard. We took turns lying on the boards and shooting video. Chris and I waded into chest-deep water, staying well in front of the big waves. When they broke, curling, ready to devour us, we'd turn, face the beach, paddle like crazy and be whisked to shore in a matter of seconds on the boogie boards by the boiling, churning mass of water and sand.

Once we were caught too close to the bottom of a huge wave as it broke. We had misjudged the curl. It swallowed us up, like a dinosaur would a slow-moving prey. We were tossed into a gigantic washing machine. All I could see was green and brown. I instinctively crossed my forearms over my forehead. It was something I was taught by Indiana. He'd told me if I ever got tossed into a big wave, the maneuver might help to prevent a neck injury if I was pile-driven head-first into the sand, which was as hard as concrete.

I'd mentioned this to Chris before we stepped into the ocean earlier that day.

Time stood still as we were embroiled in a combination of water and sand for what seemed like several minutes but was in fact, only seconds. Violently, I was thrashed around, my right ankle smashing into the ocean floor.

I prayed Chris would be okay.

I had no idea which way was up or down. I was finally rolled onto the beach, spat out by the liquid monster. I got up immediately, looking for my son, scanning the remains of the rogue wave.

I was greatly relieved when I saw Chris get up about twenty feet away from me. I ran over to him to make sure he was alright. We laughed and hugged. Other than a couple of bruises and a scrape or two, we came away from that experience with a whole new respect for Mother Nature.

It was over all too soon. That night we were back on our way home. We ate supper on the plane and slept most of the way back to Vancouver.

The next morning we drove home through snow and fog. With the grey mist swirling around us, I marvelled at how some 15 hours earlier, we were playing in surf deeper than the snow.

"Boy, reality sucks, doesn't it?" I said to my family as we watched the snow falling around us.

I mentally counted the months to Ironman, and thought of Indiana again.

Perhaps some day there will be a surf portion of the triathlon.

I should have asked for his phone number, in case I needed to brush up on my surfing.

Chapter 8

The next morning we woke and looked at each other's deeply bronzed skin.

Our Hawaiian holiday seemed like a wonderful dream.

After lunch I took off for my longest run to that point. I left the house at 3 p.m. bundled up like an Eskimo.

What a world of difference, I thought. *Two days ago we were playing in fifteen foot surf - today I'm running in six inches of snow.*

Nine miles, one hour and 24 minutes later I arrived back home. My lungs were sore from breathing in the frigid air, but I ran well. I would have felt better had I been running on a Hawaiian beach.

I was elated at having just completed a third of a marathon. I knew I wasn't far from achieving my next goal which was to run for at least two hours.

I arrived at work the following Monday morning and was soon acclimatized to winter. Back in serious training, I found the lack of heat extremely bothersome.

Again I was forced to stretch, to make sure my joints and muscles were limber. Because of the unusually deep snow which had fallen on Penticton and Kelowna, I was back on the treadmill, watching people play tennis.

I entered into another dimension of indoor training. I'd borrowed a wind trainer from Dave Bullock. The device allows one to cycle on the spot. The front wheel of the bike is removed and the front forks are bolted into a square metal frame. The rear wheel sits on a rotating drum, allowing you to pedal on the spot. I watched TV while working out on it, but like running indoors, it was a static, boring way to spend an hour cycling.

On February 5th, the weather broke and I ran outdoors. Slush was piled deep on the sides of the roads and the temperature was around freezing. I ran facing traffic, near the ditches. It was sloppy, wet and difficult. It would have been easier to run in sand-filled Jello.

It was also very dangerous. Extended mirrors from pick-up trucks whizzed by my ear muffs, only inches away as I tightroped between the traffic and the ditch. Whenever I faced an eighteen wheeler, I instinctively headed for the deeper snow to my left. I tried not to think what would happen if I slipped under the big tires. The stark reality kept my eyes wide open. My reflexes were taut, stretched to the point of reacting too quickly when I thought I was in trouble.

More than once I ended up in a foot of ice-cold water as a truck had come straight at me. I couldn't believe how many drivers didn't see me until I was right in front of three tons of steel, rubber and chrome. I felt I was a target, seen through the cross-hairs of a hood ornament. I'd witness a sudden, wide-eyed surprised look behind the steering wheel, and a quick motion by the driver to steer the truck away from hitting me.

By then I was already in the ditch.

I don't usually swear, but at those times, the air was blue. I'd quickly slosh my way back to the radio station and jump into a steaming hot shower.

Nobody told me running was a potential contact sport.

* * * * *

Winter seemed to drag. The weather reports said the Okanagan was suffering through the coldest and longest winter in 26 years. How lucky I was.

I was fighting a training depression because of the extended bitter weather.

I met Dave Bullock on a Saturday morning over coffee and I told him of my 'funk'. He said it was a common reaction for any athlete training year-round. Unlike seasonal sports, there was no down-time for Ironman. He urged me to be patient and recommended I vary my training schedule, to take away the predictability of each session. He suggested a combination of short distance, high intensity runs, then longer distances at a slower, but steady pace. I did three miles, almost at a sprint after a brief five or six minute warm-up. The following day I ran eight miles.

By the first of March I was running three miles on the treadmill in 23 minutes. I knew I wouldn't do that kind of time in the outdoors, because wind and road conditions are factors which don't enter into running indoors.

I also got back in the pool. I was juggling my work schedule with swimming on Mondays and Wednesdays; running on weekends and playing hockey three times a week.

Lunch was eaten on the run, literally, in my car and sometimes as I dressed after a game, or in the change room at the pool. The smell of mayonnaise in my ham and cheese sandwich mixed with the odor of chlorine in my nose. I was still struggling in the pool in early March when Dave Bullock told me about the 'pull-buoys' and a miracle occurred.

Pull-buoys are two cylindrical pieces of styrofoam, each, eight inches long and five inches in diameter, attached by two straps of one-inch wide strips of webbing. They can be shortened or lengthened, and when placed between the thighs or knees, they keep one's lower body from sinking. Dave told me most triathletes practiced swimming with them.

At the same time, I figured out the reason for the chlorine-burned sinuses and water filled ears. As a youngster, I'd often suffered from ear infections and I surmised my sinus cavities must have been damaged, allowing water in.

The bloodshot eyes which greeted me in the mirror after a swim, were sore. A bottle of Visene shared space with the shampoo and soap in my toiletries bag. Magically, all my discomforts disappeared when I bought goggles, nose and ear plugs.

For the first time since October, I looked forward to getting into the pool.

With enthusiasm like never before, I attacked the lanes. By the end of March, I was swimming forty lengths at a time. I began to feel more confident each time I jumped into the water. With the encouragement and tips from the lifeguards, I began to improve my stroke and time. I was doing a kilometer (40 lengths of a 25 meter pool), three days a week. My best time was 33 minutes and as encouraging as that was, I knew I'd have to knock that down to 25 minutes. There was another factor which I wouldn't experience until race day. Ironman veterans told me wind, water temperature and currents would all factor into my time. The one saving grace would be my wetsuit. They told me the buoyancy would enable me to float on top of the water.

I was hoping they were right about the wetsuit, because floatation devices are illegal in the Ironman swim. Exhilarated, I'd leave the pool on shaky legs and return to the men's locker room after each swim with increasing confidence.

One nagging thought continued to bother me. My fear of deep water. The Ironman swim course isn't parallel to the beach in four or five feet of water. I shuddered when I thought about the depth I'd be swimming in at the first turn-around, a mile straight out from shore.

It started very quietly in the back of my head.

By the time I'd showered and changed and was getting into my car, it was unmistakable - and louder.

The theme from "Jaws" would not go away.

I prayed the Ogopogo lake monster was really a myth.

As April approached, I was into my third month of two-a-day workouts, three days a week, interspersed with hockey. I was on a heavy regimen of vitamins which I took religiously throughout each day. I tried to eat at least five helpings of raw vegetables and fruits.

I was surprised at how much energy I was able to glean from them. Coming from a meat and potatoes upbringing, I had totally changed my eating habits. I also consumed a lot of pasta, rice and lean meat, usually chicken.

I was eating every two hours. My lunch container resembled a hockey bag with all the food I needed to get me through each day. It seemed like I was always munching on something, whether I was at my desk or in the car. Even though I was taking in between 4,000 and 5,000 a calories day, I often still found myself hungry.

A physiological change was taking place in my body.

My neck, shoulders and triceps had noticeably grown larger from the swimming. My waist dropped to 32 inches from 33, and my forearms were developing larger and more defined muscles. I'd sneak a peak in the mirrors in the locker room at the pool and I couldn't help but like what I saw. I was 49 years old and in better condition than most of the others.

The swimming was beneficial for my sore right shoulder. The first 10 lengths were difficult because of the shooting pains when I brought my arm up over my head for another stroke. Soon, however, the pain would melt away as the endorphins kicked in and I'd be able to do the distance without any difficulty.

I had learned to live with constant pain. Not a day went by when I wasn't sore from one thing or another. The hockey games were the toughest because of the strain on the shoulder, but I simply gritted my teeth and kept going. Each morning, I'd try to loosen up the taut muscles in the shower by stretching and letting the hot water massage the aching parts of my body. The pain was magnified if I'd banged into the boards or another player. It happened frequently as I'd skate hard for the net if I had a chance to score. It was common to be lying in a heap against the boards behind the net with a defenseman on top of me.

St. Patrick's Day was Sunday and I woke up fighting another cold. My throat had been bothering me for a couple of days. Many people at work were coughing, and blowing noses and I knew I'd caught the blast of an errant sneeze.

Even my lower bowels hurt when I coughed or sneezed and I found it difficult to get my second wind as I ran.

Spring was definitely arriving as I noticed more people running. It was still cool but, the trees were in full bud and it was just a matter of weeks before the leaves and blossoms appeared.

The hockey season ended Friday March 22nd. My cold was still bothering me, but I skated as hard as I could and felt better at the end of the 90 minute game.

Two days later, I ran the longest distance to that date. The temperature was 60 degrees Fahrenheit (16 Celsius) as I left the house after my warm-up. I ran from our house on the south side of Penticton to the condominiums in Okanagan Falls, 10.2 miles away, in an hour and a-half. I was not concerned about time, concentrating instead on distance. I started slowly and once I had broken a sweat, got into a rhythm at a constant speed. I'd asked Caroline to leave the house for OK Falls about an hour after I left home. I wasn't ready for the return run. I felt surprisingly well as she passed me after I'd entered the town and was waiting for me at the condominiums when I arrived a few minutes later.

A pattern was starting to develop which had no rhyme nor reason. I'd been getting advice from Dave and other triathlete friends about proper training schedules and how my body would react to a variety of stimuli. At times, when I felt great, I didn't swim or run as well as I felt I should have. At the same time, there were instances when I felt absolutely rotten, tired or bogged down with a cold or cough. Yet, I would perform well, or even exceed a previous best time.

On the 31st of March, I participated in the Oliver 10K run, my first organized race since a high school track and field meet in Calgary 29 years earlier. Oliver is a community of about five thousand people, 20 miles south of Penticton in the heart of vineyards and orchards.

The race start was a mile from the check-in site and finish line at a local winery. I met many friends who I knew were long-time runners and would finish much earlier than me, but I didn't care. I just wanted to do my best and finish strong. There was fresh fruit, muffins, juice and water at the registration site. Caroline and I mingled and chatted with our friends.

It was easy to let this sport get under one's skin. The camaraderie, ambiance and electricity in the air, combined to create an enormous sense of excitement.

Winter struggled to hold on as the skies were grey and the temperature was 42 degrees Fahrenheit (6 Celsius). As a warm-up, we jogged the mile from the winery to the start line. The gun sounded to start the race at 10 a.m. I was trying to stay calm and not get caught up in the excitement, but my heart was pounding even before I took my first stride. I forced myself to stay at the back of the pack, knowing the vetrans would've run me down.

We ran on a mile of gravel before the pavement. At that point, most of the others were in the distance, head of me. I fought back the feeling to push myself harder.

The combination of the excitement, the coolness and difficulty of running on something other than a treadmill was taking it's toll. Before I knew it, however, it was over. I turned the corner and was heading up the long half-mile driveway of the winery to the banner which read, 'Finish'.

Suddenly, my throat tightened and tears welled up in my eyes. I could see the electronic numbers on the portable time clock which had just turned to 55 minutes. I saw Caroline standing with Dave Bullock who had already finished. In a blur of color and emotion, I crossed the finish line and into their arms.

I was choking in the emotion of having completed my first race in almost three decades.

This was far more significant than my second place finish in the Calgary track finals in the 100 yard dash in 1967.

We hugged and laughed. Other friends came over and congratulated me.

My official time was 55:58, about five minutes slower than I wanted to finish. However, I was buoyed by the fact I hadn't hurt myself and I wasn't the last runner across the finish line.

I quickly showered, towelled off, got dressed and re-joined Caroline and our friends. I wolfed down a couple of muffins, a banana and apple with lots of water.

During the drive back home I reflected on the race. I admonished myself for not running faster. Caroline cautioned me not to be too hard on myself. She reminded me that many of the participants had been running for decades. I mused about my performance and chuckled out loud, "for an old guy, I guess I did okay".

Caroline nodded in agreement.

A half hour later we drove up in front of our house. For a moment I sat behind the wheel staring into the slate grey, late morning sky. I smiled.

The elephant was another bite lighter.

Sixth month of
chemotherapy
- no hair
no eyebrows,
no mustache.

August 1994

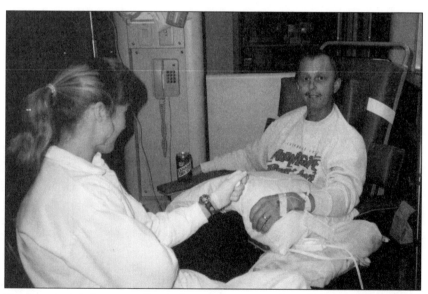

Tanis administers my final chemotherapy, after 8 long, hard
months.

October 1994

In Training,
running from
Okanagan Falls to
Penticton.

August 1996

6am, Ironman morning 1996, eating my porridge, 1 hour before
the swim start. I'm visualizing my task.

6:55am,
minutes
before
the start.

I'm reflecting
on
what I'm
about to do.

Out of the water
after one hour,
42 minutes

Struggling uphill.

The infamous
7 mile long
Richter Pass.

Hangin' on tight down the backside of Richter.

As I leave for the run saying *Good Bye* to the man who saved my life, Dr. Jack Chritchley.

Walking along Eastside Road with my son Chris, his friend Lindsay and Peter Diggins (703) who helped me finish.

Peter and I struggling about 10 p.m. to make it through
the 26.2 miles.

Slapping hands with many people at the final triumphant steps to
the Finish Line.

Dave Bullock celebrating with me behind the Finish Line.

My family, Jodi, me, Caroline & Chris.

Is this a grin or grimace?

Nothing
more to say.

Chapter 9

Caroline and I celebrated our 24th wedding anniversary on April first. It was sunny and warm, the daytime temperatures forecast into the high sixties Fahrenheit (19 Celcius).

I was a bit sore from the run in Oliver but I felt much better having beaten the cold and flu. The following Sunday April 8th, I attempted a 16 mile run from our house to Okanagan Falls town limit, and back. I ate my usual multigrain porridge one hour before I began. I packed two Powerbars and a banana in a fanny pack which I clipped around my waist to the front. I filled a large sports bottle with Gatorade and a second one with water, which I placed into holders and strapped behind me. I packed a pair of thin wool mitts and a head band in case it got cold.

I looked like an Ironman rambo, weapons on and ready for running.

It was 66 degrees Fahrenheit (18 Celsius) when I hit the streets after a 10 minute warm-up. There was a mild breeze from the south. The trek back home would be easier with the wind at my back. I was emotionally, mentally and physically prepared for the run which I hoped to complete in two-and-a-half hours.

The first hour flew by. I constantly nibbled and sipped. I sloshed through the occasional reminder of winter as I had to skirt around several large puddles of water on the highway from the melted snow. I counted 8 Ironman mile markers. They are painted into the asphalt in one mile increments to let the triathletes know how far into the run they are. It was beneficial to live in the city of the triathlon because I could train on the marathon course.

The second hour was tougher as my knees and thighs began to get sore. To my benefit, I was no longer facing the wind as I headed back home. I didn't slow down, however. I maintained a constant speed in spite of my discomfort. Two hours, forty minutes later I arrived back home. I had finished all the food and water a half hour earlier, but felt fine. I hobbled up the front stairs and into the house. I threw together a triple ham and cheese sandwich and devoured it in four bites. I gulped down a large glass of milk and hit the shower, satisfied with the long distance run.

With spring firmly entrenched, I spent more time on my bike. One of the favorite training routes was to Summerland, a community of ten thousand people, eleven miles north of Penticton on Highway 97. Groups of cyclists could often be seen on weekend mornings heading out of the city.

An incident occurred on Saturday April 13th which sobered me up quickly to the potential dangers of Ironman training.

Dave Bullock was also preparing for Ironman and I often worked out with him. I'd only done a half dozen short distance rides before the two of us struck out on that Saturday morning.

Thirty minutes later, at the bottom of the two mile long Summerland hill, we turned right along the lake, toward Shaunessy's Cove, a small bedroom community east of Summerland. This popular triathlon training route leads to Peach Orchard Road, a very steep one-and-a-half mile hill at the far end northern outskirts. It is a major test of stamina. Standing on our pedals all the way, we arrived at the top 10 minutes later, puffing and red-faced. We paused to gulp some water and rest for a few minutes before the trip down the long, two mile curve to the bottom, and home. At the summit of the Summerland hill, Dave joked, "us big, heavy guys can go a lot faster downhill than you short, skinny guys". Dave weighed about 200 pounds and was six feet tall while I was 157 and 5 feet 9 inches in height.

We didn't need to pedal down the highway. He slowly edged away from me as we picked up considerable speed. The wind roared through my helmet. My eyes teared up from the blast of air. With eagle eyes, I looked for anything that could knock me from my bike. Bits of glass flashed in the sunlight, and small rocks streaked by me as I riveted my eyes on the shoulder of the road about a hundred feet in front of me. Cars and trucks blew by me on my left. The semi-trailer trucks created a vortex of air which seemed to suck me in. I leaned to the right to maintain control of my ten-speed. The concrete barriers on my right were only a couple of feet away as my hands squeezed my handlebars in an iron grip. Bits of debris and sand ricocheted off my sunglasses. The bike began to wobble as my speed increased. I pumped my rear brake ever so gently. I fought a feeling of panic. I was uncomfortable at the high speed. A locked up wheel would catapult me into the chasm on my right, or under a wheel to my left. I was conscious of a continuous roar of vehicles as they came up behind me, then disappeared out of sight around the bottom of the mountain as the road turned right Dave had disappeared around the curve. I finally made it to the bottom. I blinked to clear the dust in my eyes.

Seconds later I came upon a horrifying sight.

Dave was lying under his mangled bicycle half-way into the right-hand driving lane.

The dust was barely settling as I squeezed both brakes simultaneously and skidded my bike to a squealing halt beside him. His helmet had been split in two but he was conscious. His elbows and knees were bloodied. He groaned when I asked if he thought any bones were broken. In pain, he said he didn't think so. I asked him to lie back and try to relax as I tried to flag down a motorist for help. Moments later a man in a Volvo station wagon stopped in front of Dave's crumpled bike and came running over. Seconds later, a B.C. Environment officer in his truck stopped behind us and turned on the red and blue emergency flashers behind the cab and ran to us. I was glad he was there because many vehicles zipped by us at 60 miles (100 kilometers) an hour, only a few feet away.

I told the officer what had happened, and he quickly got back to the truck and radioed for an ambulance.

In the meantime, Dave had sat up and was holding his left arm in his lap. He grimaced when he tried to move it and said his shoulder was very sore. The skin on the fingertips of his right hand been ripped off when he hit the asphalt. The ambulance arrived within a couple of minutes and the paramedics put Dave inside and took him to the Summerland hospital. The environment officer offered me a ride to Penticton. We loaded the bikes in the back of his pickup and he drove me home. We removed the bikes and I thanked him. As he drove away Caroline came out of the house and asked what happened.

Her eyes widened as I recounted the spill. She asked if I was okay and then inquired about Dave. I told her I was going to go back to the hospital, pick him up, and take him home.

In minutes I'd put both bikes in our garage and was back on my way to Summerland. Dave had just come out of X-ray where it was discovered he'd suffered a separated shoulder. They'd already bandaged up the cuts and bruises.

"Road rash hurts like hell," Dave said through clenched teeth as we left the hospital. He walked slowly and groaned as he got into my car.

On the way back he told me how fast he was going when he'd lost control. "Forty miles an hour, mate," he said. I spun my head around and stared at him.

"What!" I said, stunned. I let out a low whistle.

I had him back home in twenty minutes and wished him well.

"Don't go riding without me", he joked.

In somber silence I drove the short distance home. I knew I had to be careful on my bike from that moment on, but I also had to put the accident behind me and continue to train as hard as I could.

I clenched my teeth. *The elephant could bite back.*

Chapter 10

The following Saturday April 20th, I rode the 50 miles (80 kilometers) to Oliver and back. It was cool when I left at 9 a.m. but I knew the midday sun would be very warm so I dressed in layers.

I pedaled along East Side Road toward Okanagan Falls. The road was becoming intimately familiar to me. There are several rolling hills just before town which are taxing when running or cycling.

The road south between OK Falls and Vaseaux Lake is a narrow, four mile stretch of two lane highway. There are no shoulders. I rode on the white line separating the driving lane from broken asphalt, gravel and sand on my right. Cycling on this rough, uneven surface was difficult when on a bike with racing tires the diameter of one's thumb. I felt the reverberation of every pot hole and stone through my arms, neck and head. A deep hole caused my teeth to rattle.

I shared the road with coupes, pick-ups, vans, recreational vehicles and semi-trailer trucks. They passed me, sometimes only inches away. The narrow section ended at the north end of Vaseaux Lake. From there, a wide, smooth shoulder greeted me, and I sped up.

I often came upon cyclists in training. We waved even though we were unknown to each other. Most were dressed in skin-tight cycling apparel in bright hues of iridescent colors. Many were also on state-of-the art triathlon bikes with clip-on pedals. They allow the cyclist to pull up on the pedal stroke, increasing the efficiency, and gaining more speed and power.

I looked down at my baggy old sweatpants, and pedals with straps around an old pair of sneakers.

I decided to invest in a pair of proper cycling shorts and clip-on pedals and shoes.

I wasn't sure about the rainbow-colored clothing, however. I don't look good in anything with more than one color. I'm conservative in my politics, thinking and clothing.

The day was breathtakingly gorgeous. Just before Oliver I passed the first of many orchards. The blossoms were in full bloom. White and pink petals sparkled brilliantly in the sunlight as far as I could see and the sweet smell was overwhelming.

At Oliver I rested for 10 minutes, drank lots of water and munched on my fruit bars and a Powerbar.

I'd learned my lesson and was well prepared. I had three bottles of fluid with me and was constantly sipping and eating. I filled up the bottles at a service station and left for home.

Ironman training, which started at the first run, was an ongoing journey of new experiences and discovery. I learned what I could do, how I could improve and what my limitations were. My body responded well to some new concepts but rejected others. Leaning over the handlebars with my torso parallel to the top bar for several hours at a time, was part of the learning curve. I had to train myself to eat while in motion. I'm prone to a lot of burping because of my hiatus hernia. I discovered the fine line of eating just enough at the right time

So I nibbled and sipped constantly.

I arrived back home about noon, weary, but happy I'd done the ride in a good time, without getting run over by a logging truck.

On the next ride to Summerland, I discovered one of the most interesting and physiological occurrences which male cyclists often deal with when spending long periods of time in the saddle.

I had just passed the spot where Dave had his accident, about sixteen miles into the 26 mile round trip.

I was effortlessly pedaling at 20 miles an hour with the wind at my back. Leaning forward, my hands on the aerobars and thumbs intertwined. I suddenly felt something strange in my genitals - a lack of sensation.

All feeling seemed to have left my body at that point on my posterior which was in contact with the seat.

Alarmed, I quickly sat up straight, grabbed the top of the bars and wiggled my butt.

I reached down with my right hand and grabbed my crotch. Nothing!

The feeling was gone, numb, like hitting your funny bone in the elbow.

I wasn't sure if I should be alarmed or laugh. I'd never had frozen private parts before, except maybe in a blizzard on the prairies; but that's a different story.

I was intrigued. What should I do?

I began to appreciate the humor in what I was experiencing.

How to get life and the feeling back between my legs was my immediate quest. I decided to discretely massage the afflicted area in such a way that oncoming motorists would not know, or see, what I was doing.

Looking around me I began to gingerly squeeze my crotch until some of the feeling began to return. My eyes were focused on the traffic whizzing by me in both directions.

Wouldn't it be lovely if a mother with her young kids in a mini-van saw what I was doing and drove into the lake trying to shield young eyes from my actions?

The mental picture I'd just painted made me laugh. The more I thought about it, the louder I laughed. A couple of days later I talked to some of my triathlete buddies and then to my doctor who told me it was a normal occurance in male cyclists.

A pelvic nerve runs through the area and when compressed by the weight of the body on the narrow, hard seat for long periods of time, causes the loss of feeling to the genitals.

I though this might have some kind of medical or scientific possiblities but couldn't quite figure out how. I was told female cyclists don't suffer this type of discomfort.

Much of my training gave me a perspective on how my attitude was as important as the training. As April ended and May arrived, I realized I could only attain a certain level of achievement given my relatively short period of training. Many Ironman triathletes my age had several finisher certificates on their walls and I knew I didn't dare dream of trying to keep up with them during training, or the big day itself.

I had to train only to the maximum for my physical conditioning, not someones else's. The chemotherapy less than two years ago had taken it's toll. I was fighting more than just building muscles and endurance. I knew the discomfort in my joints from the chemotherapy would take years to subside - if ever.

At almost 50 years of age, I had to let the 20, 30 and 40 year old athletes pass me by on race day. I could not attempt or force myself to exceed my capabilities to stay with them, much less, even think of passing them.

My only goal was to earn my finisher's medal, regardless of how long it took. Unlike hockey, which I'd played all my life, this was my first attempt at anything of this magnitude.

I vowed to concentrate on building up my endurance as much as I could and then do my best on race day.

The spring weather turned ugly for a couple of weeks in early May making training difficult. Wind, sleet, short periods of snow then sun, made biking and running interesting. I was either over, or underdressed, freezing or cooking.

My neck was often sore because of the cold wind. Constant leaning over the handlebars, head up, was a strain. My elbows were only eight inches apart on the pads on the handlebars which stretched the shoulder blades. I again went to massage therapy several times to alleviate the stiffness.

On Sunday May 10th, I participated in the annual Apple Blossom 10 mile run in Penticton. We left the start area about a mile north of the Naramata turn-off heading toward the finish line at the Sicamous paddlewheeler in Penicton.

The Naramata road is one of the most scenic in the Okanagan, It was overcast with sprinkles of rain and the sights and smells of the orchards permeated the moist air. The narrow two-lane highway undulates and has many curves with degrees of difficulties not found on flat road coarses. I knew this was good for increasing my endurance. Along the way I met up with a fellow who was a real inspiration. We introduced ourselves and I listened to his remarkable story.

Fifteen years earlier he was almost killed in a car accident. Permamently disabled, he had taken up running as part of his physical therapy. He ran with a limp and his left arm was almost useless, flopping at his side. I was awed by his determination and promised myself again to never quit until I reached my goal.

We chatted about kids, marriage, work and our respective philosophies on life.

As I was jogging smoothly beside him and his awkward shuffle, I became more amazed by how I was taken away from my own training difficulties and was deeply admiring of his courage.

In a drizzle we arrived at the finish line together in one hour and 37 minutes. I thanked him for his company and told him how inspired I was by his story. I shook his hand goodbye. I told him I would not forget our run togther.

Later that night Caroline was watching TV and "Touched by an Angel" came on.

I sat up, ram-rod straight in my chair.

Could it be he was like an angel, sent to inspire me?

Chapter 11

The swimming was progressing well. My best time was 64 minutes for eighty lengths, just over half the swim course distance. I calculated the time would get me out of the water in two hours, about 20 minutes ahead of the cut-off time. I was elated.

I had tried bi-lateral breathing as recommended by a lifeguard, which is breathing from both the left and right as I stroked through the water. It was cumbersome because I found myself concentrating on counting strokes, instead of practicing proper technique.

I decided to stay with what was comfortable, breathing from the left side only.

My first long-distance race was Sunday May 19th; the Kelowna Marathon.

Most runners were entered in the full 26.2 mile marathon but I didn't want to take a chance of injury so I'd registered for the second option, the half-marathon.

Caroline and I got up at five that morning, made coffee and arrived at the race site just after six a.m.

I had my breakfast in a thermos which I ate along with a banana and some orange juice. I was surprised at how uptight I was. It was the thought of starting in a pack of more than 600 other runners and that my competitive nature didn't allow me to do anything less than my best. I didn't want to sprain or pull a muscle or ligament. The thought of injuring myself with only a few months before Ironman did not sit well. My goal was to run hard, yet not over-extend myself.

I didn't have to carry my bottle holder around my waist because there were plenty of aid stations along the route. I did load up with a couple of Powerbars and fruit snacks.

Milling about just before the gun sounded was even more nerve-wracking. Caroline waved to me from the sidewalk and I smiled back. I met several friends who were running and we chatted about the race.

At 7 a.m., the sharp crack of the starter's pistol signalled the beginning of the marathon. I let most of the runners pass me and didn't get going for three or four blocks. Within a couple of miles, however, I had broken a sweat and was running comfortably. Like Penticton, Kelowna is a beautiful city. The route took us through parks bordering on Okanagan Lake and residential areas. Trees were in full leaf and there were still remnants of blossoms on some of those bearing fruit. The morning sky was clear with the temperature near 68 Fahrenheit (18 Celsius). I was passing runners, while others passed me. The ebb and flow, the fluidity of the race became evident. It was as if the run had taken on a life of it's own, like a gigantic creature with 1200 legs all in motion at different speeds.

At the quarter mark of the 13 mile event, I looked up and saw what looked like a human gazelle dressed in yellow hurtling toward me. He was gone in a flash, long legs looking like they were taking 20 foot strides. I looked at my watch and saw I'd been running for thirty minutes.

I found out later this human dynamo won the half marathon.

I shook my head and tried not to be intimidated. The morning sun quickly became warm and I took off my T-shirt. Underneath was a sleeveless undershirt with my race number pinned on. I wrapped my outerwear around my waist. It flapped as I ran, like a skirt.

Time passed quickly as I met and greeted a number of runners. At the ten mile mark, my calves began to hurt. I lengthened my strides for a while in an effort to stretch the muscles, ligaments and tendons, trying to keep them loose.

As I neared the finish line, I realized the decision to only run in the half-marathon, was wise.

I wasn't ready for the full distance. I looked at my watch. It showed 1 hour 57 minutes. I could hear the voice of Steve King, the popular triathlon and marathon announcer, as he named each finisher and did a brief description of their prior running or triathlon accomplishments.

Steve was known as the 'voice of Ironman'.

I tried to quicken my pace to try to make it under two hours but my legs did not respond. I rounded the final turn at the park entrance and saw the "Finish" banner dancing in the breeze. I looked at my watch again.

1:59:30.

I knew I couldn't make it, but pushed my legs as hard as I could.

When Steve recognized my number he quickly told the crowd of runners and spectators about my cancer battle. I got choked up again. I crossed the tape in 2 hours, one minute and 23 seconds. Caroline was there to give me a hug. She said I stunk and we laughed. I told her we'd have to keep the car windows open all the way home because there were no showers on the site.

I got my finishers medal, had something to eat, and we drove home.

The following weekend saw us in Salmon Arm, a city 100 miles north of Penticton on the beautiful Shuswap Lake. I participated in my first ever triathlon. Even though it was a mini-event, it would still give me the experience of 'transition'; from the swim, to the bike, then the run. I had practiced going from biking to running over the past several weeks. My legs felt like concrete each time I stepped from my bicycle, and it took some time before I could run without difficulty. The Salmon Arm mini-triathlon would be a good test in telescoping the three events together.

The swim portion was 30 lengths in the indoor pool. The bike portion covered 12 miles and a three mile run finished the trithalon.

I struggled to complete the swim in 22 minutes. It seemed as if all the stroke and breathing training went out the window. I was caught up in the excitement. Swimming in a narrow lane only six feet wide with three others felt confining, restrictive.

I constantly saw kicking feet and flailing hands through the churning water in my goggles. When I got out of the pool, I changed into my cycling gear in the mens change room. Many of the competitors had run straight to their bikes and began the cycle portion.

My legs were wobbly as I got on the bike, but they soon recovered and I rode strongly through the course back to transition. I changed quickly into my runners and took off. As before, my legs felt heavy and I fought off the feeling of lethargy. I pushed hard and came across the finish line in one hour 29 minutes.

Caroline had been sitting with my brother and his wife. Surprised by my finish, she asked me to go back a hundred yards so she could take a picture of me crossing the finish line.

As we drove back home, we talked about the experience. I told her how alarmed I was at the difficulty I experienced in the pool. I reasoned it was because of the close confines of the others and my lack of experience in competitive swimming.

I was troubled about that for several days after. Back in the pool during my lunch hours, alone, I swam strongly and confidently. I knew I would somehow have to psyche myself up to get ready for another mini-triathlon in Kelowna, and the Olympic distance Peach Classic triathlon in Penticton five weeks before Ironman.

A thought jolted me. If I had trouble in a pool with a handful of swimmers, how would I react to a lake swim with 1,700 triathletes?

Over the next several weeks I concentrated on my swimming. If I wasn't able to get out of the lake before the cut-off time, the rest was strictly academic.

I increased my riding and concentrated less on running. My goal at Ironman was to jog one mile, then walk the next and repeat the process until I made it to the finish line. I expected to complete it in five hours. Near the end of May I swam 100 laps in the pool in 1 hour, 13 minutes, which was encouraging. This distance was two-thirds of the swim course. For every minute I took off my time, it was one more I could spend on the bike and run.

On Saturday morning June 21st at 8 a.m. I took off for Osoyoos on my bike, 45 miles south, for a four hour ride.

Near Oliver, half-way to my destination, a brutal head-wind forced me to turn back after an hour. I headed back north toward Penticton with thoughts of pedalling to Summerland. There, a wall of rain five miles north, forced me back to Penticton. The sky was dark, rain-filled and ominous to the north-west, but sunny to the south-east.

I planned to cycle back to Penticton, then to Naramata and home. I had plenty of food with me as well as Gatorade and stopped several times to fill up my water bottles.

I cycled into a head-wind again to Naramata, 10 miles north of Penticton and finally returned back home at 12:07 p.m, weary, sweaty and sore.

My butt was raw from the ride. I'd purchased a new pair of cycling shorts and found out the hard way, it's not wise to wear underpants.

I'd also learned it's wise to apply plenty of vaseline to the privates and bum to prevent chaffing and soreness. I winced at the thought of all that guk in my pants.

It was still a struggle to force-feed myself lots of fluid while riding. Mick Kelly, a friend who had done several Ironman races before, constantly reminded me to drink as much as I could. He'd told me he'd once been unable to finish one because he hadn't consumed enough water.

A monumental breakthrough occurred on Wednesday June 26th.

I did the full Ironman distance in the pool, 150 lengths in one hour, 55 minutes. I was elated!

This was THE pivotal moment, because I knew I could complete the swim portion of Ironman before the cut-off. I visualized tearing the albatross of swimming which was like a millstone around my neck, and flinging it as far as I could.

I ecstatically told Caroline and the kids about my accomplishment at supper.

The reality of crossing the line at Ironman became more clear, more in focus. Thousands of times over the last few months I had finished the triathlon in my mind. The visualization was crucial in programming my body to finish. With the swim time conquered, the image of breaking the tape caused me to become emotional. I choked back tears.

Visualization had helped me through the chemotherapy two years earlier.

The same mental discipline would help me to achieve my Ironman goal.

Chapter 12

My confidence continued to balloon. On Sunday July 14th, after a big breakfast of porridge and juice, I left the house at 9 a.m. to ride the full 112 mile bike course.

Dave Bullock offered to join me even though he was recuperating from his spill a couple of months earlier. He was still hoping to compete in the triathlon and this ride would tell the tale.

I was in my cycling shorts, filled with Vaseline and wore a short sleeved cycling shirt. I was loaded up with bananas, Powerbars, fruit snacks, bottles of Gatorade and water which I'd re-fill whenever they were empty.

I'd bought a pair of cycling shoes which clipped to the pedals. It took some time to get used to the tightness of the shoes, unlike the old sneakers I'd been training in.

Caroline covered my shoulders and back with sunscreen. After a good-luck kiss, I clipped my shoes to the bike pedals and took off.

The Ironman Canada triathlon bike route is infamous because of the Richter Pass, just south of Osoyoos. It's an uphill, eight mile killer stretch of highway to the top of the pass. The route then goes north through Keremeos, Yellow Lake, Kaledon and south again to OK Falls. From there the route headed north on East Side road to the finish line.

It was another gorgeous day filled with sunshine. Afternoon temperatures were forecast in the mid 90's

Fahrenheit (high 30 Celsius) range. I knew I'd be okay as long as I drank lots of fluids.

By noon we'd cycled past Osoyoos and were on our way up the Richter Pass.

It was blazing hot, and the slow pedal up the monster hill caused the sweat on my forehead to flow freely. I often blew the perspiration away from my mustache and was bothered by the salt which was stinging my eyes. I sipped continually from one of the water bottles and shot some of it into my burning eyes to wash away the sweat. Without stopping, we reached the summit twenty-nine minutes later, and took a ten minute break to catch our breath.

My thighs felt like they were on fire from the lactate acid which had built up in the muscles. I stretched my back to get rid of the stiffness. My neck was aching from keeping my head up.

I ate another Powerbar, took a shot of Gatorade and washed it down with several gulps of water. Dave guessed at our estimated time of arrival back home.

"It's just after 12 noon," he said, looking at his watch. "If all goes well, we should be back between 3:30 and 4."

"That would make it about a 7 hour ride," I noted.

He nodded his head. "If you can maintain this time on race day, you should do quite well. The pro's do it between 4 and 5 hours. You'll be okay." He winked at me in encouragement.

There was a downhill leg from the pass about five miles long which kept my attention riveted on the road.

At 40 miles an hour, we coasted down the hill. I was looking carefully for any small objects on the shoulder which could catapult me under a car or truck.

Dave's crash was still vivid in my mind. At the bottom of the hill, the muscles in my entire upper body including my fingers were taut from the death-grip on the handlebars. As the road levelled off, I constantly wiggled my torso, neck and fingers to try to loosen up the stiffness. The following 30 mile stretch of road from the pass, through Keremeos to Yellow Lake was rolling highway.

Near Keremeos, Dave told me he wasn't sure if he would continue. The injuries from his crash were making it difficult for him to cycle much longer.

We stopped at a nearby fruitstand to take a breather and to refill our bottles.

After a few minutes he told me, " you're going to have to carry on by yourself, mate." He paused and I could read his disappointment. The two months of lost training had taken their toll.

"I'll get a ride home," he said.

"Before you continue on", he added, "I've got something to give you". He went to his bike and removed his plastic drink container which was attached between the handlebars. From it protruded a long, thick plastic straw. "Fill this with Pepsi, let it go flat and you'll find it great for instant energy."

I gave him a punch in the shoulder, went into the store at the fruitstand and bought a pop. I asked the clerk how hot it was. She walked back to the back door to a large thermometer hanging on a nail. "108 Fahrenheit," she called back, adding "that's 42 Celsius."

I whistled through my teeth.

"Holy smokes" I said to her, "that's hotter than I like."

I knew I'd be drinking a lot of water and flat pop the rest of the way.

I took off my cycling shirt. Two thin straps going over each shoulder held my cycling shorts up.

I never went longer than 10 minutes without taking a drink. I dumped a generous amount of water over my helmet every second or third swallow to keep my head cool. Near Yellow Lake, the road again went uphill for four miles. I stopped at a campground when I reached the lake and filled up my water bottles again. It was risky circling around the lake on the narrow two-lane highway with only a couple of feet of shoulder on which to ride. To the left, cars and trucks passed close enough to kiss; to the right just beyond the two-foot high concrete barriers, it was 50 feet straight down to the water.

Again, I had a death-grip on the handlebars. Half-an-hour later on Highway 3, I was at the junction of Highway 97; Penticton to the left, Okanagan Falls to the right. I took the right exit and in 15 minutes was in town and headed back north toward home on East Side road.

At 3:40 p.m., I arrived at my front door. It had taken me six hours and 40 minutes to complete the 112 mile trip.

I felt surprisingly well as I walked up to the front door and said "hello."

Caroline greeted me. Her wide smile instantly transformed to a look or horror. She put her hands up to her mouth and gasped, "look at your shoulders," she exclaimed. "you're burnt to a crisp!"

I hurried to the bathroom and took down the straps of my cycling shorts. The white outline contrasted sharply with the pink and red skin on my shoulders and back.

She got some salve, tenderly applied it to the sunburn and sympathetically hoped I could sleep that night. As I lay on my stomach, my mind was still speeding along the highway. I wondered again how successfully I could put the three Ironman elements together. I felt comfortable in the water, and was confident I could complete the bike route before the cut-off.

The marathon would be *the* major challenge.

At work the next morning, my back was on fire. Just before my first sales call, I walked into a nearby walk-in clinic. I waited to see the doctor, a pleasant man in his forties. He whistled through his teeth when I took off my shirt. "You've done some damage," he said examining the blistered, bright red skin. "Looks like you were riding." I told him about my Ironman training.

He congratulated me and gave me a small container of expensive salve containing silver which he said would reduce the painful effects of the sunburn.

"I'm treating you for a first-degree burn." he said. "Apply this for a week and it should be better by then." I thanked him and left.

I didn't train for the next two days giving my painful upper body a chance to repair itself.

I also registered in my first major triathlon.

The Peach Classic is held in Penticton each July. It attracts many elite triathletes from around the world. It's an Olympic distance event consisting of a one mile swim, 25 mile ride and 6 mile run.

It would be my first real test in the water.

I had rented a wet suit for the race. Two days before the triathlon, on the evening of July 19th , I stood on Okanagan beach and put on the rubber suit. It felt constricting. I had difficulty breathing, because the wet suit was skin-tight, especially around the ribs. However, I was most concerned about the ability of the suit to keep me on top of the water. I prayed I wouldn't sink. I walked into the lake, my stomach in my throat. I felt the coolness on my bare feet and ankles as I walked into waist deep water. I was pleasantly surprised at the insulating factor of the thin rubber. When the water was at my chest, I dove in.

I came up instantly, sputtering, coughing and trying to suck in huge volumes of air. It felt like an anaconda was wrapped around me. I walked back onto the beach and began to pull up the rubber from my lower body as I'd been instructed to provide more expansion of the wetsuit on my upper body, mostly to the chest.

Again I dove in. It didn't feel as tight. I felt better and swam parallel to the beach in about five or six feet of water. I was extremely relieved when I found myself on top of the water. The wetsuit gave me much more floatation than the pull-buoys did.

My confidence mushroomed. I began to stroke strongly. I swam from the Peach concession stand to the S.S. Sicamous, an 1800's paddlewheeler permanently moored on the southwest corner of Okanagan Lake, two-thirds of a mile away.

I almost shouted for joy when I swam into shallow water at the bow of the old ship and walked up on the sand. Caroline waved at me from our car. I peeled off the suit and towelled myself dry.

"I did it - I swam in the lake", I said excitedly.

On the way home, however, reality hit me again. The swim course was not along the shore. I would have to swim straight out from the beach for a mile, then back.

Sober second thoughts tempered my initial elation.

At seven o'clock on Saturday morning, July 21st, the gun sounded to begin the 1996 Peach Classic.

I purposely waited until I was the last of the three hundred triathletes in the water for the one mile swim. In the distance, a half-mile away on the sparkling sun-lit surface of the lake, sat the large white houseboat which was the turn-around point of the swim. I walked into the water which was churning as 600 arms and legs stroked and kicked.

I dove in and stood straight up again.

Gut-wrenching panic hit me like a sledge hammer to the midsection.

The water in front of me suddenly seemed like an insurmountable obstacle. The elephant I was riding was on it's hind legs, rearing violently in the air, it's screeching, trumpeting deafening in my ears. It was blotting out the sun of confidence which shone so brightly on me just two days ago.

I screamed at myself, *GET IN THE WATER - YOU'LL BE OKAY - YOU WON'T DROWN!*

I dove in again. Awkwardly my arms flailed like out-of-control windmills. My feet kicked furiously, spraying water all around me. I ingested gulp after gulp of lake water. My breathing rhythm was non-existent. I fought to maintain control of my mind and body. I continued to scream at myself to relax, to get into a nice easy swimming stroke, like I'd done for so many thousands of lengths in the last half year.

Never in my life, including the time of my cancer diagnosis had I ever been that frightened. I forced myself to relax, to calm down, to remember what I had learned.

I counted; *one, two, breathe; one, two, breathe; one, two, breathe.* When I exhaled underwater, I tried to keep my forehead up out of the water and my eyes on the houseboat a half-mile away instead of looking down.

As quickly as it hit, the panic washed over me like the warm lake water, and was gone. I realized I wasn't sinking.

I looked down and couldn't see the bottom any more. The waves of sunlight penetrated the water to a depth of perhaps ten to twelve feet. Beyond that was a greenish-brown haze.

I CAN DO THIS. I CAN SWIM!

I ordered my arms to swim harder and I felt myself moving quickly through the water.

Suddenly, in front of my goggles, a pair of bare feet appeared, furiously moving up and down, creating a multitude of bubbles which gurgled in my ears. I had caught up to another swimmer. I moved to the right and in a couple of minutes passed the swimmer.

YAHOO!

I swam harder.

Before I knew it, I was at the houseboat. I had passed several other people. Around the turn with a half-mile to go, I turned it on. I was delirious with joy. I was swimming in a major triathlon and was passing others. A smack in the nose from a heel brought me back to attention. I had swum into another person. I could see the large red balloons along the swim course and the beach in the distance. Below me, the murkiness began to get lighter and soon a dozen feet beneath me, I saw the rocks in the sand. I wasn't far from the finish line.

In no time, I touched the beach with my fingertips. I stood up and walked quickly through the gate where my number was recorded as having finished the first leg of the triathlon.

Again, I heard Steve King's voice in the distance as he recounted once more to the spectators, my cancer journey and of my determination to complete the Ironman.

I HAD DONE IT!. I KNEW AT THAT MOMENT, I COULD FINISH THE IRONMAN SWIM!

I had a smile on my face a mile long for the rest of the triathlon.

I finished in three hours, 14 minutes, about an hour longer than the winner's time. I didn't care. I had taken the biggest and most crucial bite out of the elephant. The swim course had knawed at me for months and I'd felt a shot of acid into my stomach everytime I looked at the lake on my way to work. Although I still had a lot of swimming to do, I had defeated my greatest adversary.

I HAD CONQUERED THE LAKE!

On Saturday July 27th, less than a month away from Ironman, I attempted again to run to Okanagan Falls and back home. Caroline agreed to be my mobile aid station. We placed a five gallon plastic container full of water into the back of our compact station wagon, along with a couple of towels, enough food for a small army and some first aid supplies.

I drank a bottle of water before I left the house and asked her to leave about a half-hour after me.

At 3:30 p.m. when I left the house, it was 103 degrees Fahrenheit (39 Celsius). I took off in the mid-day heat because I wanted to simulate the time I expected to be leaving transition. I revelled in the hot afternoon. Heatwaves shimmered on the street in the distance as I headed south. I was slathered with 30 SPF sunblock and was wearing a cap above my sunglasses.

I ran easily for the first couple of hours. Caroline had joined me and was driving ahead of me in two mile increments, parking where she could along the narrow two-lane, mountainous road. At each stop, I approached the car, gobbled down some food and drank as much water as I could. On the turn-around from Okanagan Falls, I took off my cap and wrapped a small towel around my head like a turban and soaked it with water. It helped in keeping me cool. At 6:30 that evening, I told Caroline I'd had enough. I'd made it within four miles of our house. I'd run almost 20 miles. I was satisfied with my effort and was confident I would be at the finish line about 10 o'clock on Ironman night.

Two weeks before Ironman, I participated in my final mini-triathlon in Kelowna. I knocked seven minutes from my time at Salmon Arm that Sunday morning. It was my final tune-up for the big day.

I again met with Dave Bullock over coffee at our house and discussed the final preparations for Ironman. Dave told me the rest would be a mental journey of staying confident.

"You must also get as much rest as you can from now on", he also warned me, and added, "it's too bad you can't get the week off work". I'd been at my job less than a year, I didn't qualify for holidays.

He told me to do as much training in the lake as possible rather than risk injury on the bike or by running with just a few days left to go. I'd heard horror stories of triathletes getting hit by a car, or spraining an ankle just before the race.

He grinned and said to me, "at least I know you're not gonna drown."

After he left, I was immersed in a jumble of thoughts.

"How can I get enough sleep?" I pondered.

I realized the upcoming two weeks could well be the most crucial time in the previous eleven months of training. Mentally, physically, and spiritually, I had to be functioning on a level I'd never experienced in my life.

If one of these elements was lacking, I might not complete my dream.

Only one journey in my life had paralleled this one, my cancer journey two years before.

I smiled and promised myself, *until Ironman, I will stay away from trucks, cars and anything bigger and heavier than me that can cause injury.*

Chapter 13

On Sunday August 18th, one week before Ironman, I woke at 4:30 a.m. to complete the full 2.4 mile swim. I wanted to simulate race day morning so my body would know what to expect.I prepared my usual amount of porridge and put it in a thermos. I brewed a strong cup of coffee and drank it in the car as Caroline and I drove to the lake. My wetsuit was wrapped in a large towel.

The sun was just rising over the eastern mountains as we arrived at the beach where the swim starts. We sat in the car for a few minutes, each lost in our own thoughts, staring at the large body of water into which I would dive in one week along with the other triathletes. Several ducks and Canada geese wandered aimlessly back and forth near the water in front of us. Small birds chirped and swooped from the trees in the boulevard beside us. The lake lay like a mirror. There was no wind.

It was an idyllic, picture-perfect Okanagan morning.

We chatted occasionally, killing time. The mountains on the west side of the lake slowly came to life as the sun rose. Forty-five minutes later, at 6 o'clock, I opened my thermos and dumped some brown sugar from a small plastic pouch into the wide-mouthed container holding my still steaming break-fast.

I ate it slowly, being careful not to burn my mouth. I also drank two glasses of orange juice.

At half-past six, we got out of the car, opened the tailgate to our station wagon and I took out my wetsuit. We walked toward the sand on the grassy part of the area just before the beach. I took off my sandals and peeled off my sweat pants and top. In my swim trunks, I suddenly felt the cool morning air. It sent a shiver up and down my spine.

I quickly stepped into my wetsuit and rolled it up my body. It was one size larger than the one I used in the Peach Classic and it felt much more comfortable. I had plenty of room for chest expansion. My feet started to get cold from the dew on the grass so we walked to the sand. I looked at my watch; it read 6:42. Caroline zipped up the back of the wetsuit and I spent a couple of minutes adjusting it until I felt comfortable. The stillness of the morning was broken by several other triathletes who'd arrived to do the swim.

I talked with a man from Toronto who was training for his sixth consecutive Ironman. He and his family took their yearly holiday in our town.

I dove in for a ten minute warm-up. The water was surprisingly warm. The wet suit felt perfect and I swam along the beach for a hundred yards or so and turned around.

At seven a.m. sharp, I pushed off from the start area toward the S.S Sicamous. My plan was to swim to the boat and back, three and-a-half times which was the full Ironman distance.

I was full of confidence and swam strongly, parallel to the beach in about seven or eight feet of water. Several dozen others were doing the same.

I was startled by the first fish which swam beneath me, close enough to touch.

At 8:45, I finished the swim and walked up to where Caroline was sitting. My legs were wobbly and I felt as if I was falling forward.

I peeled off the wetsuit and dried myself. I looked back at the lake and saw there were even more swimmers in the water.

Tourists had arrived at the beach and were setting up for what promised to be just another day in paradise.

I placed the towel on the seat and sat down. I looked at Caroline and said, "I *WILL* finish the swim." She gave me a kiss and a hug.

On Monday August 19th, I didn't swim. I was on a different roller coaster of emotions as I had to face another challenge - my future in sales. I knew I was headed for a career change. I shook my head, as if to fling out those negative thoughts. I didn't need the mental struggle a week before Ironman.

For the next five days, I knew I'd be going through the motions at work. I had to devote every single waking moment to visualizing completing Ironman. Every second had to be spent getting mentally prepared, fortifying my armor of confidence and attitude - to not allow anyone or anything to crack that invisible wall of security. There was no room for one sliver of *I think I can*, or *I hope I can*. I had to put every single ounce of my heart, body and soul into believing, *I know I can*.

I knew my work would suffer, but I had no choice. I could deal with my future after the race.

I swam short distances Tuesday through Friday in the pool. I forced myself to be in bed each evening at 8 p.m. I concentrated on keeping my emotions in check and visualized being calm at all times.

On Saturday morning, the day before Ironman, I did another one hour swim in the lake, then took my bicycle to the transition area and checked it in. At 11 a.m., Caroline and I attended the compulsory triathlete meeting on the grass in front of the bandshell at Gyro Park, near the finish line. The rules and regulation were spelled out by race officials. Looking around me at 3,000 athletes, spouses and friends I drank in the emotion and excitement associated with Ironman Canada. People from all over the world were in Penticton for an event which would change lives and challenge participants, especially first time triathletes like myself, to discover their ultimate threshold. There was a story to be told in each person who was there.

I knew when I came across the finish line the following day, my life would never be the same again.

I spent the rest of the day relaxing. Life-long friends Carol and Rome Thibert and their son Corey arrived from Lethbridge to cheer me on. We spent a couple of hours after supper getting ready for the morning. I'd made a checklist of everything I needed and laid them out on the living room floor.

I was ready.

Caroline and our friends went out for the evening and I went to bed.

I listened to the Eagles "Peaceful, Easy Feeling", several times. I revelled in how relaxed I was. Other triathletes had told me they were so uptight before the race they couldn't sleep the night before

I drifted off about 9 p.m.

My plate was just about clean.

I was down to the last few bites of the elephant.

Chapter 14

At four in the morning, Ironman race day, the alarm went off.

I jumped into the shower, dried off and got dressed. I made a pot of coffee. Caroline, Chris and Jodi were soon up and joined me in the kitchen.

They were members of 'Ironcrew', part of the 4500 volunteers at each Ironman in Penticton. My family had asked for assignments inside the finish line. I wanted them to be there when I crossed the line.

It brought tears to my eyes thinking of us hugging each other in a victory celebration.

Before we left at quarter to five, we held each other in a small, tight circle. We thanked God for strength, and for my family, solidly standing behind me through the struggle with cancer and the very turbulent year we'd faced. We were thankful for our faith, family and friends. The emotional moment was a tremendous boost.

We looked through misty eyes and gave each other a kiss and extra squeeze.

We arrived with our friends at the Ironman site just after five o'clock. I said good-bye and prepared to get myself numbered.

In the semi-darkness, I took off my sweatshirt and a volunteer wrote my number, 999, on both upper arms and outside calves on my legs. We were given two Velcro wrist straps with our numbers on them. These would be removed from us after finishing the swim and bike portions as proof of having completed them.

The Ironman site was a tented city with very strict security. Tall portable fences had been erected surrounding the area covering several acres. The transition area was neatly laid out in a manner that allowed the triathletes to go from the swim, to the bike and then to the run course.

Long, tall racks with corresponding athletes numbers containing their transition bags were in strategic lines for easy access.

In my first bag were my cycling shorts, shoes, gloves, cycling shirt, Vaseline and sunglasses. My second bag contained my running shoes, shorts, underpants, socks and T-shirt.

A third and fourth "special needs" bags with our numbers were taken by Ironman volunteers early that morning, halfway to the cycle course, and at the 13 mile mark of the marathon.

In my third bag was a bottle of very strong Gatorade and several Powerbars which I would pick up on my bike. At the turn-around of the run, my fourth bag contained another bottle of Gatorade, more nutrition and a sweatshirt. I knew I'd need it later that night when it would be cool.

There was a tent each for male and female triathletes who wanted to spend a few minutes changing for each leg of the race. The professionals competing for money and others who were trying to beat their previous best times went straight from each event to the next without taking a break. Since I wasn't going to be in the hunt for any prize money nor did I have a previous time to beat, I planned on taking my time in transition.

Daylight arrived by six a.m. I sat on a curb in the bike compound, my breakfast in my thermos. A steady stream of people and bicycles passed in front of my eyes, but I was soon alone in my thoughts. Again, I replayed the Ironman race in my mind. I visualized myself coming out of the water with plenty of time before the cut-off. Then I was on my bike, cycling hard. In my runners, I came across the finish line, pumping my arms in victory.

Just as I'd beaten Hodgkin's disease, I'd conquered the Ironman.

"Good luck, mate."

I snapped out of my daydream. Dave Bullock was there with his hand out. I grabbed it and gave him a big hug and thanked him for all of his time training with me.

I finished my porridge and went to put on my wetsuit. It was 6:14. I still had about a half-hour before my warm-up swim.

I put some anti-chafing cream on my neck, underarms and the back of the knees where the rubber would be the tightest to prevent the skin from being rubbed raw. I slowly and deliberately put on my wetsuit, which by that time fit comfortably.

At 6:40, I stepped into the lake for the warm-up. The water temperature was 70 degrees Fahrenheit (20 Celsius). I put on my bright yellow Ironman swim cap, inserted my earplugs, put on my nose plug and slipped on my goggles. I swam straight out and back. The lake was teeming with black rubber suits, arms, legs and yellow caps. I felt strong, comfortable and confident. Back at the beach, I paused and looked over the sea of swimmers. Almost 1,700 athletes would soon be churning through the swim course. I was wise enough to know it would not be a good idea for me to be near the front.

Ironman swimmers seed themselves, especially the pros. The faster ones were at the front, which made a great deal of sense to me. Getting swum over, clawed, smacked and kicked in the face, stomach or other assorted body parts, was not my idea of a good time.

I decided to get near the back of the horde.

I heard Steve King's voice in the background warning swimmers to get behind the start line as it was almost time to begin the race.

I quickly ran up the beach one more time to the fence and gave Caroline and the kids a kiss and hug.

At seven a.m. sharp, the old cannon boomed to officially start the 1996 Ironman Canada Triathlon.

Like horses in the gate, raring to go, the fastest swimmers were at the front, chomping at the bit. It took a couple of minutes before I could dive into the water as the athletes began to spread out. The first leg of the swim course was just over a mile long straight out to a houseboat. Huge orange balloons tied together, several hundred feet apart, guided the way.

There were dozens of kayaks and canoes on both sides of the course to keep swimmers on course.

I felt great and swam strongly.

I could see the sun's rays dancing off the splashing water in front of me. Yellow caps bobbed up and down. Arms were flailing everywhere. I could hear the gurgling water as it washed past my ears each time I took a stroke. Millions of air bubbles created by this human washing machine in the green-brown hue were boiling around me. I was being tossed back and forth, up and down, by the wave action created by the hundreds of bodies in my area.

I had some idea of time without looking at my watch. As I neared the houseboat at the turn-around, I knew I'd been in the water about a half-hour. I took a second to look at my watch and I was right on the mark for the first mile at 36 minutes.

The boat loomed large as I began the wide turn to the left. I could see the bottom of the hull under the water.

Something there caused me to lose my stroke and momentum.

Divers are strategically placed underwater throughout the course to help any swimmers who may be in difficulty. I saw two below me at the bow of the boat. One was upright, holding onto the anchor rope. The other, just below the first diver, was parallel to the surface of the water as if he were lying on a sofa. His hands were behind his head, fingers intertwined, holding onto the rope, and his legs straight out, ankles crossed and flippers pointing skyward.

I started to laugh. This is not good when your face is in the water. I sucked in a mouthful of water. Sputtering, I lifted my head up, treaded water for a few seconds, cleared my throat and got back into my swimming rhythm. I sneaked a look below me as I got to the back of the boat. He hadn't changed position.

From that point, there were 450 meters before the final left turn back to the beach. The course resembled a long, narrow triangle.

In the home stretch, I could see the beach less than a mile away. I felt terrific. I was swimming efficiently, barely turning my head to the left, just enough to clear the water to breathe. I reached as far as I could with each stroke, bringing my arms down in a big arc, to pull on as much water as I could.

I counted five more big red buoys, then four, three, two and finally I had reached the last one before the finish line. I could see faces now behind the line just a couple of hundred yards away.

As in the Peach Classic, the water began to lighten up as it got shallow. I saw the bottom which quickly rose up to greet me.

I finally touched sand.

I HAD DONE IT! I HAD COMPLETED THE IRONMAN SWIM!

I felt the same euphoric joy as I did five weeks before. I stood up in thigh-deep water and found myself floundering on unsteady legs.

I removed my earplugs. A wall of noise boomed into my consciousness. I lifted my goggles up to my forehead and let out a loud whoop.

I looked at my watch. Again I let out a yell of delight.

It read 1:42:20.

I screamed a *"YYYEEEESSSSSSSSSSSSS!"*

I stumbled through the gate where a volunteer ripped the Velcro band with my number from my wrist.

The training had paid off in spades. I made a bee-line for my family. They were wearing wide grins when I ran up to them and gave each a hug over the fence. Tears of joy had smudged the mascara on Caroline's face. There would be many times during the day when her makeup would take a beating.

They asked how I felt. I gave a 'thumbs up', and said, "fantastic". I told them I'd be back in about seven hours, after I'd finished the bike course.

I left them and quickly ran into the transition area. Two volunteers asked if they could help me out of my wetsuit. I said "sure", and laid down on the grass. They pulled down the two-foot zipper and peeled the suit from head to feet as one would a banana.

As I moved through the entrance to transition, I stopped cold in my tracks. My jaw hit the ground.

There in front of me was the man who saved my life.

Chapter 15

Wearing his perpetual grin and as large as life was Dr. Jack Chritchley.

Dripping wet, I ran to him, gave him a bear hug and lifted him off his feet. I thanked him for being there. He'd recently left his practice in Penticton to work at the B.C. Cancer Agency in Vancouver.

I quickly picked up my transition bag containing my cycling gear and he walked with me to the mens' change tent. We chatted constantly. He asked me how I felt and I told him I was on top of the world because of my time in the water.

"Barring any injury, there's no way I won't finish," I bubbled back at him.

There were a couple dozen other men changing as I sat on a bench. While we got caught up with events in our lives, I dried off and was dressed to ride within 10 minutes.

I stood up, hugged him again and told him I'd be back about 4 o'clock.

I grabbed a juice box, a banana and muffin, and headed for my bike. On the way, I stopped at the booth where people were administering sun block to the athletes. I was determined not to get sunburned again. A volunteer applied liberal amounts to any exposed skin and gave me a small container of SPF 30 which I could apply later.

I quickly walked to the bike transition area and saw that the majority of triathletes had already left. It didn't matter because I had triumphed over the most difficult part of the race for me, the swim. I knew I could complete the other two disciplines of Ironman. I looked at my watch. It was 9 am. I ate with one hand and walked my bike to the start of the bike course with the others. I felt groggy, still trying to find my land-legs.

Hundreds of spectators were waving and cheering for each athlete leaving transition. I looked for my family and friends who had taken their places on the bleachers and we waved to each other.

As I cycled up Main Street, more groups of spectators were arriving with folding chairs under their arms. People I didn't know, shouted encouragement as I passed them, picking up speed and shifting gears.

The support for Ironman Canada is unrivaled anywhere, including the world championships in Hawaii. Over the past week I'd spoken with many athletes from around the globe who had continually heaped praise on the local organizers because of the thousands volunteers who help out each year.

It is the envy of the other nine official Ironman races on the globe.

The route through the middle of Penticton was closed to traffic and I was able to shift into high gear quickly. In minutes I was out of the city heading south on a road with which I was very familiar. There were cyclists in front of and behind me, in a long strung-out line.

I was smiling. I couldn't get over the fact I was cycling on the bike portion.

I pinched myself to make sure it wasn't a dream.

My cycling shirt flapped in the wind. Water dripped from the back of my hair onto my shoulders. I looked at my watch: 9:10 a.m. I got my elbows and fingers onto my aerobars and settled in for the 112 miles ahead of me. I rode in the shadow of East Side Road, cut into the mountain. I shivered in the coolness as the sun had not yet climbed high in the sky to throw it's rays on me. In no time, I cycled through Okanagan Falls as I had on so many training rides over the past few months; then past Vaseaux Lake, and onto the flat stretch of highway to Oliver. Again, as I had been over hundreds of hours of training, I was deeply immersed in my thoughts. All the thinking, planning and dreaming would come to a climax in a dozen hours. I'd dreamt of everything and anything; from little insignificant thoughts to what I'd like to do with the rest of my life.

There was one profound thought, which stood above all.

I was alive and well, and participating in an event, which two years ago, was impossible to comprehend.

I tried to reason why I was participating in the Ironman race, and not lying in a grave.

Why was I alive; why did other cancer patients succumb to this insidious disease?

There was no answer.

I wouldn't second guess what God had done for me and gave thanks for the strength and faith I had to get me to where I was on a gorgeous late August morning.

I smiled. I was going to have fun finishing the race.

As the sun climbed higher in the sky, the temperature shot upward. As they'd been forecast all summer, temperatures would be scorching. I decided not to take off my shirt regardless of the heat.

There were water stations every five miles along the bike route and I chugged as much water as I could. My goal was to complete the ride, one aide station at a time. It was easier to get my head around five mile increments, instead of a single 112 mile journey. I continually munched on pieces of Powerbars and bananas which were available at the stations. I was well stocked with fruitbars which I carried in pockets on my cycling shirt.

At eleven o'clock I pulled into Osoyoos and prepared myself for the long, brutal climb of the Richter Pass just up the highway. Fifteen minutes later, I was at the base of the pass and geared down for my journey up the eight mile monster.

I looked up and shouted, "LET'S DO IT!"

A steady stream of cyclists, in single file disappeared into the clouds at the top of the pass as I shifted into a lower gear.

I opened my mouth, took a shot of water and dumped the remainder of the bottle over my helmet. It was so hot, I never flinched at the cooling sensation. Ahead of me, I saw the first of two aid stations, about a mile up the four lane highway.

Heat waves danced on the hot pavement as I looked through sunglasses streaked with evaporated water and sweat. I pedalled strongly, never slowing down except to grab a bottle of water handed to me at the stations. I checked my watch. It had taken 22 minutes to climb it, eight minutes quicker than during the practice run. In spite of the water, I was overheating when I reached the summit and sucked in large amounts of air. Not stopping, I got ready for the downhill side of the Richter Pass.

I took another gulp of Gatorade and placed the bottle back into it's container on the bike. I leaned forward, grabbed the lower portion of the curved handle bars and pushed down hard on the pedals.

As in my training, I held on for dear life as my bike streaked downhill. The broken white lines melted together as they flashed under my tires. I couldn't hear the traffic because of the noise in my helmet.

The highway continued to undulate to Keremeos. Two triathletes, a man and a woman, several miles apart were standing forlornly in the ditch to my right with flat tires. I soberly glanced at them, thankful my bicycle hadn't broken down. I knew a small piece of glass or a broken chain could add significantly to my time. A major repair could mean disaster.

I tried not to think of that possibility. Near Keremeos, just past the half-way mark, I picked up my first special needs bag which contained my second bottle of Gatorade. I'd finished the first one and threw it into the bag. I took a big gulp, put the bottle in the holder after placing the empty one in the bag. They would be returned to transition when all the cyclists were back.

I constantly fought the stiffness in my body from being bent over the handlebars.

The ride was becoming tedious by the time I reached the four mile climb to Yellow Lake. Although not as long as the Richter Pass, it is equally as tough, because of the ninety miles already completed. Permission was granted by the Ministry of Highways to close one lane of the narrow highway around the lake. As I neared the top, I could hear a commotion. A female volunteer was holding a flagperson pole with "stop", on one side and "slow" on the other. A line of cars and trucks were standing still waiting for traffic from the other side to subside.

A rather large man was objecting at having to stop his car and was giving the woman a rough time. As I rode past, a burly Ironman helper came to the rescue of the beleaguered volunteer.

I wanted to stop; to tell the motorist to get a life and not have a heart attack.

Around the lake and on another series of rolling hills, I continued on.

Suddenly without warning, I felt a sharp, stabbing pain on the outside of my left knee. It jolted me out of my seat. I stood up on both pedals. Then just as quickly, it subsided. I exhaled quickly and continued on. A few minutes later however, the stabbing sensation returned, knifing it's way into the center of my knee.

I tried not to panic. *It'll go away soon - it HAS TO GO AWAY!*

The pain intensified as the miles rolled away under my triathlon bike. I couldn't push down on my left leg. My shoe was clipped to the pedal and was simply going for a ride. I would have to propel myself back to transition with only my right leg.

A stab of horror shot through my body.

What if I can't run?

I violently shook that ominous thought from my head and thought of only one thing.

Get through the ride - we'll deal with the run later!

At the junction of Highways 3 and 97, the pain was stabbing to the point where I became frightened and wasn't sure if I could continue.

Down the long hill to Okanagan Falls, I coasted and snapped my cycling shoe out of it's clip and began the arduous task of trying to relieve the pain in my knee.

I flexed the muscles, stretched the leg as much as I could while at the same time keeping my eyes on the road, cars and the ditch.

At the bottom of the hill, I clipped the shoe back into it's place on the pedal and tried to push. The pain was still there. I knew something was dreadfully wrong. Other cyclists began to pass me. I looked at my watch. It was four o'clock. I should've been back in transition.

Cut off for the bike portion was 5:30 p.m. I had 10 miles to go.

I firmly set my jaw, squeezing my teeth together. I was not going to quit. I hadn't gone through a year of training, sore muscles, cold and heat to give up.

I thought again of my cancer and chemotherapy.

I pushed down hard on the pedals.

Fighting the throbbing pain, I arrived at transition at 4:38. I had less than an hour to spare. I wondered how much time I'd lost because of the injury.

I hobbled off my bike and the volunteers removed the second Velcro strip from my wrist. I limped my bike back to it's place in the racks in transition.

Caroline and the kids suddenly appeared and excitedly congratulated me. They sobered quickly when I told them about the knee. Dr. Chritchley arrived shortly and also shook my hand, but his smile disappeared when I told him about the injury. He led me to the medical tent where dozens of physicians were volunteering their time. He asked Caroline and the kids to wait outside.

"Sorry," he apologized, "but we've got a lot of people in there and we just don't have the room." They said it was okay.

Jack summoned an orthopedic specialist whom he knew and the doctor carefully examined my knee for 10 minutes, constantly asking questions as he put my leg and joint through several contortion exercises. There was significant pain which made me cry out when the leg was stretched to the left.

"Can you run on it?", he asked. I got up and walked to the opening of the tent. I took two quick steps and felt a searing flash in the center of the knee. I fell forward, using my hands to break my fall. The joint had given out.

His question had been graphically answered.

I was helped up, and hobbled to the chair I'd been sitting on. The doctor consulted with Jack and told me he suspected a stretched knee ligament. He said it wasn't a serious injury but we had to decide if I should continue.

The blood drained from my face. Panic welled. My stomach tightened. I felt ill.

"NO!" I said with firm determination.

Hot tears stung my eyes. I wiped them off with a towel.

I told Jack, "I can't disappoint my family and friends..." I paused, "...and I WON'T disappoint myself."

I looked at my watch. It was 5:17. I'd lost three-quarters of an hour in the medical tent.

I stood up and said, "Jack, I'm going for a walk - a bloody long walk".

Chapter 16

Dr. Chritchley expertly wrapped my knee with a tensor bandage, to support the injury as much as possible. One of the other physicians gave me four Tylenol tablets and wished me good luck.

Jack said, "I drove up last night to be with you today and I have to leave soon for Vancouver. I must be in my office first thing in the morning. I wish I could stay to watch you come across the line".

"I'll call you in the morning to let you know how I did," I promised.

I embraced him again and held him tight for several seconds. He was a very special man.

He put his hands on my shoulders, stared me straight in the eyes and said, "you can do it," he told me in that gentle, but firm and reassuring tone which he'd used often during my chemotherapy.

"Gotta go," I said. I had to get out of there before I got choked up.

I put on my Canadian Cancer Society baseball cap, waved good-bye to Dr. Chritchley, kissed and hugged my family, and promised I'd be back before the midnight cut-off.

Every step hurt as I left the medical tent on my 26.2 mile journey.

I checked my watch. 5:25 p.m

I walked as quickly as I could past the cheering crowd and back up Main Street where almost 9 hours earlier, I was pedalling my bike.

The winner, Thomas Helriegal of Germany, had already crossed the finish line more than four hours earlier and picked up his cash prize. I was just starting the marathon. Many other triathletes were coming back to the finish on the other side of the road. I swallowed hard. I again vowed to be back to get my finishers medal.

Fifteen minutes later, near the middle of the city, I caught up with another triathlete who was limping, favoring his right leg. I didn't know it then, but meeting him was the final, pivotal moment in putting my cancer journey behind me. From watching my first Ironman triathlon in 1994, in the middle of my chemotherapy, to participating two years later, I was writing the final chapter in my metamorphosis.

I introduced myself and we shook hands. His name was Peter Diggins, an Australian who was working for the Saudi Arabian government as a map-maker.

We discussed our injuries and decided to help each other through the marathon. We checked our watches. It was a quarter to six. We did the math. To get back about 11:45, we would have to walk at four miles an hour.

We shook hands to reaffirm our commitment.

We picked up our pace. A sporadic stream of runners and walkers heading back to transition gave us 'thumbs up', or 'high fives' if we were close enough to each other and encouraged us.

Peter and I chatted about ourselves, families and life experiences. I told him about my cancer journey and why I was doing Ironman. He'd done a couple of other Ironman races around the world and was doing his first Canadian event.

We marched out of the city and along East Side Road. We checked each mile marker which was stenciled on the pavement on the right side of the road. At the pace which we'd established we were doing 13 minute miles, slightly quicker than we needed to.

"How's your leg," I asked.

"It hurts like hell, but I'll live," he grinned at me.

"Same," I said, emphatically, "and, Peter, *we are GOING TO DO THIS!*"

Our conversation slowed as the sun slowly dipped behind the mountains to our right, across Skaha Lake. It was still very warm, but I knew once darkness fell, it would cool off considerably. I'm glad I packed a sweatshirt in my special needs bag which I'd pick up at the half-way mark. We continued our forced march with military-like precision, our steps in unison. Peter and I were the same height. Often it sounded like there was only one person walking.

We reached the northern outskirts of Okanagan Falls about 7:30 at the ten mile indicator. Dusk was slipping away to darkness. We drank water at each of the aid stations, a mile apart. The friendly, encouraging volunteers made us feel good. Cheerful best wishes rang in our ears as we left each station behind.

I told Peter my knee was beginning to throb at each step and I knew I was doing more damage every time I put my foot down.

"Keep going - you can get it fixed later," he said, grinning.

We laughed. I was so thankful we were able to keep a sense of humor in our journey through pain. I was surprised at the number of triathletes who were still coming and going. I'd had visions of Peter and I walking forlornly by ourselves in the dark.

At 8:30 p.m., we passed through OK Falls and were at the turn-around. We had walked 13.1 miles in just under three hours.

The temperature had started to drop so I put on my sweatshirt. The crew at the half-way station encouraged us not to give up.

"Okay, my friend," I said to Peter. "We're homeward bound."

We turned to each other, put our hands up and high-fived each other. We'd only stopped for a couple of minutes but I could feel the muscles in my thighs and calves begin to tighten. For the first time, I noticed how sore my toes and the balls of my feet were.

I shrugged off the discomfort, and we again picked up our pace.

As we headed back to transition, the evening began to slowly develop into a surreal, dreamlike vortex of pain, numbness, anxiety, determination and discovery. We walked mechanically, as if we no longer had control of our legs. The mutual pain we shared was masked by the briskness of our strides. It was the ultimate journey of mind over matter.

Yet as difficult at it was, neither of us ever considered aborting our mission. We were feeding off each other's lock-jawed determination to keep going.

We marched along in total silence, each of us deeply immersed in our thoughts when the true meaning of Ironman struck me.

The event was not one of celebrating the victories of the chosen few, who with God-given physical endowment, enabled them to complete the 142 miles of madness in eight or nine hours.

It was instead, a test of human determination which mortals like Peter and I, and countless thousands before us, had chosen for very specific reasons to attempt, and finish.

Each of the seventeen hundred people in the race had a story to tell about why they were doing Ironman.

I decided to quit philosophizing and keep myself focused on what I had to do for the next couple of hours.

Near Skaha Estates, 16 miles into the marathon, I felt the discomfort in my shoes increase dramatically. It felt as if some of the small pebbles from the sand and gravel shoulders of the road had found their way into my runners.

I told Peter I had to stop for a moment to take off my right shoe to shake out the sand and rocks. I sat down on the shoulder, untied the runner, removed it and the sock. I shook them both out, put them on and tied up the runner. I tried to get to my feet.

My legs did not respond!

In those few seconds, they had stiffened up. Close to panic, I hollered at Peter to give me a hand. He was 30 or 40 yards ahead of me by that time. He quickly jogged back and grabbed both of my outstretched hands and forcefully yanked me to my feet.

I took a step. My feet felt like they were embedded in concrete blocks. My legs, shaky and weak, trembled as I attempted to get them moving again. In the darkness, I'm sure my complexion had turned white from fright. I told him I could not stop again in spite of the pain, or discomfort. Within a few minutes I had shaken off the effects of the near-disaster, and we were back to our regular cadence.

The blackness of the night descended. At the seventeenth aid station, we were handed several glo-sticks which emitted a soft green light. They were surprisingly bright in the blackness. In the distance we could see the lights of Penticton shimmer as they reflected and danced in the mirror-like calmness of Skaha Lake.

The old saying, 'so near, yet so far' was never more prophetic than at that moment.

We substituted warm chicken broth for water as the temperature dropped. It was soothing and provided nourishment.

Ambulances passed us, then returned after retrieving those who had 'hit the wall', and could not continue. Each time I saw the red flashing lights coming our way, I again fortified my resolve to not be a passenger in an emergency vehicle that night.

The RCMP and St. John Ambulance were also patrolling, lending assistance where they could. Peter and I counted down the aide stations. There were pockets of supporters camped along the way, yelling support to every athlete who passed by. We thanked them for their support.

Again the magic of Ironman manifested itself. Strangers greeted strangers, and became friends.

From behind, a beam of headlights illuminated the road in front of us ,and we heard a car honk. It was Caroline and the kids. They had been searching for us, wanting to make sure we were okay. She got out of the car and Chris got behind the wheel. For a short distance she tried to keep up, but couldn't match our brisk pace.

I gave her a quick kiss and said we'd be at transition between 11:30 and midnight.

She got back into the passenger seat and as they drove away, Chris gave us a quick toot of encouragement. The tail lights disappeared in the distance.

What a boost!

We looked at our watches. It was almost 9:30. Eight more miles to go. I felt like I was walking on a pathway of needles. Sharp, stinging sensations ripped through the numbness of both feet. I bet Peter I had blisters forming or breaking on the bottoms of both feet. He said his felt the same way.

Time both stood still, and was fleeting. We seemed to be walking forever. The lights of the city didn't seem to get any closer. Yet, the seconds and minutes ticked by and before we knew it, another hour passed. At 10:30, relentlessly charging ahead, we had almost arrived at the city limits. Peter and I looked at each other and smiled.

Four more miles to victory.

We passed the marina to the left. It was almost eleven o'clock. Just over two more miles to the finish line.

When we passed our neighborhood on South Main Street at Dauphin Avenue, a wonderful surprise greeted me. Our neighbors had erected a huge cardboard sign about eight feet tall which read, 'Ironman Wally, we're proud of you'. They waved and cheered as we passed by. Some of the kids ran to us to slap hands.

Suddenly in the glare of flashing red lights ahead, we saw a poor soul lying partially in the street as we approached the intersection which joins South Main and Main Street.

Paramedics were attending to an unconscious athlete. I shouted if he was going to be okay and the attendant said, yes.

We looked at our watches. 11:17. One more mile to go.

We knew we'd be in just after 11:30.

The lights down Main Street stretched to the Penticton Lakeside Resort Hotel on Lakeshore Road. The finish line was one hundred yards to the left on the T-intersection at the front of the hotel. Small groups of spectators still sat on bleachers or on chairs on the sidewalks, clapping as we strode by.

"Pete, I can't believe it - all these people still here at almost midnight," I exclaimed. He nodded in agreement.

"We did it, man!" I shouted when we were a few blocks away. We both shook hands and hugged as best we could at four miles an hour.

We could hear Steve King's voice on the P.A. as we got closer.

All those hundreds of hours in training had paid off. The pain and discomfort ravaging my body disappeared. I couldn't feel a thing except an emotional exhilaration which was bursting inside me, welling up like an enormous surfing wave. I was choking up again as I had in each of the races over the past few months.

Since last October, I'd run this Ironman thousands and thousands of times in my mind.

Each time I crossed the finish line, weeping.

Two blocks to go. The cheering of thousands of people at transition got louder. We could see the glaring lights at the finish line through the trees of the park where the bandshell was.

Peter had insisted I go ahead of him when we got to the end of the street. He said he would hold back. I objected, wanting to cross the line together, but he held up his hand. He wanted me to cross the line by myself.

We turned the corner.

The huge white Ironman Canada structure was a football field distance away. I could see Steve King on top of the archway, under which each triathlete ran through the finish tape.

It was like seeing the brilliant, blazing light at the end of the tunnel.

In seconds, the metamorphisis would begin.

My breathing suddenly became difficult and my throat constricted. I was overwhelmed at what I was about to accomplish.Through swimming eyes, I saw the long "Ironman Canada Finisher" banner stretched across the line, held by a volunteer at each end.

The fences holding back the spectators had long since been removed.

I jogged the last hundred yards.

A long line of hands on both sides were stretched out to me in the narrow five or six feet opening which snaked to the finish line.

Again I heard Steve's inimitable voice, packed with the emotion of the moment, *"...and now ladies and gentlemen, this is number 999, a local man who has conquered Hodgkin's disease and has now conquered Ironman Canada to become a finisher. Mr. Wally Hild......"*

His voice faded as the cheers got louder. I slapped hands on both sides of me. Everyone was smiling, some people were wiping away tears. Suddenly, it was there as big as life - as big as an elephant - the twenty foot high Ironman Canada finish line structure.

In a whirling kaleidescope of sound, motion, colors and emotion, I crossed the finish line, pumping my arms in victory.

I ran through the wide tape which wrapped around me to affirm I had completed Ironman.

I bawled openly, gagging, trying to get enough oxygen. I was choking in my tears which were streaming down my face, blurring the scene before me.

I had never experienced that kind of emotion, ever.

Winning the Stanley Cup could not hold a candle to the exhilaration I experienced.

Moments later I was encircled by my family, in a tight embrace like the one we'd shared twenty hours earlier that morning in our living room.

We clutched each other, tears mixing with sweat. I thanked God for my family, my friends and life.

In a blitz of activity, I received my Ironman Canada Finishers medal from Judy Sentes, the Ironman Canada Race Society Past-President. Michael Campbell, the current President and his wife, Beth, presented me with my Finishers T-shirt.

Moments later, I saw Dave Bullock. I briefly pulled myself away from my family, ran to him and gave him a big hug. He lifted me off my feet. I thanked him for his time, encouragement and faith in me that I could finish the race.

Graham Fraser, the owner of Ironman Canada congratulated me as did Kevin MacKinnon the Communications Manager of the race, and many others who had followed my story.

I hugged Peter Diggins, who was an enormous part of my finish and thanked him for his physical and mental support. My official time was 16 hours, 34 minutes and 17 seconds.

I hobbled into the medical tent and had my feet checked. I had blisters the size of two-dollar coins on the bottom of both feet with smaller blisters behind each toe.

Lying on a table a short time later, a volunteer massaging my aching legs, I could see the outline of the Ironman finish structure through the trees.

It no longer looked formidable like in the race which had been playing in my mind countless thousands of times in the previous eleven months.

As my friend Ian Mandin had told me, 'you can eat an elephant one bite at a time'. So it was with Ironman.

The fireworks exploded into the inky-black sky at midnight, signalling the end of the 1996 Ironman Canada Triathlon. Flashing pinwheels, streaking, multi-colored blasts of light, lit up the sky. I accepted it as my personal victory finale. This was my celebration of an event which would profoundly change the direction of my life. Nothing could stop me from accomplishing anything I wanted. Nothing!

I had reached my goal, one step, one stroke, one pedal-push, one minute, one hour, one week, one month...

one bite at a time!

You are a child of the universe,
no less than the trees
and the stars ...
you have a right to be here.
And whether or not
it is clear to you –
no doubt the universe
is unfolding, as it should.

(Desiderata)

ORDER FORM

Books & Videos available from Wally Hild and
lightSPEED MULTIMEDIA INC. :

Yes, I would like to order _____ copies of :
From Hodgkin's to Ironman (the book) @ *$11.95 each* _____
Faith, Family and Friends (the book)
- release date December 1999 @ $11.95 each _____

PLEASE ADD 7% GST AND $2.50 PER BOOK SHIPPING AND HANDLING.

Send cheque or money order to:
    Wally Hild / Circle of Light Motivational Experience
    2636 Roblin Street,
    Penticton, B.C.,
    CANADA.
    V2A 6H4
    Phone: (250) 493-8376
    Fax: (250) 493-0825
    Email: Hild@vip.net
    Wally Hild available for motivational speaking.

Master card and telephone orders accepted.

Yes, I would like to order _____ copies of:
From Hodgkin's to Ironman (the video) @ *$25.00* ($31.82 incl. S&H and all taxes) ea.
Institutional @ *$19.95* ($26.45 incl. S&H and all taxes) ea.

Send cheque or money order to:

    lightSPEED MULTI MEDIA INC.,
    201a - 311 Main Street,
    Penticton, B.C.,
    CANADA,
    V2A 5B7.
    Phone: (250) 493 - 8191
    Fax: (250) 493 - 8174
    Email: lightSPEED@img.net

Master card and telephone orders accepted.